Pink Floyd

Pink Floyd

Album by Album

Stephen Palmer

WHITE OWL

AN IMPRINT OF PEN & SWORD BOOKS LTD.
YORKSHIRE – PHILADELPHIA

First published in Great Britain in 2026 by
White Owl
An imprint of Pen & Sword Books Limited
Yorkshire – Philadelphia

ISBN 978 1 03612 927 9

A CIP catalogue record for this book is available from the British Library.

Typeset by Mac Style
Printed in the UK by CPI Group (UK) Ltd, Croydon, CR0 4YY.

The Publisher's authorised representative in the EU for product safety is Authorised Rep Compliance Ltd., Ground Floor, 71 Lower Baggot Street, Dublin D02 P593, Ireland.
www.arccompliance.com

For a complete list of Pen & Sword titles please contact:

PEN & SWORD BOOKS LIMITED
47 Church Street, Barnsley, South Yorkshire, S70 2AS, England
E-mail: enquiries@pen-and-sword.co.uk
Website: www.pen-and-sword.co.uk
or
PEN AND SWORD BOOKS
1950 Lawrence Road, Havertown, PA 19083, USA
E-mail: uspen-and-sword@casematepublishers.com
Website: www.penandswordbooks.com

For Hal & Wendy

Contents

Acknowledgements

Thanks to: Rob Andrews, Ron Bourley, Alan Busby, Jon Champignon, Oz Hardwick, Hal Harries, Jo Lashly, Garry Masters, James Tansley, TITCH (Bernard Holcroft), Aidan @ Tubeway Records, Ed Zep (Edzep11), all my friends at Bill's Kitchen in Ludlow, and all my Bluesky and Facebook friends.

I would also like to thank Jon Wright, Olivia Camozzi-Jones and Charlotte Mitchell at Pen & Sword Books, and Mélanie Dangereuse de Clegane.

Introduction

One night when I was about fifteen, I put a cassette of *The Dark Side Of The Moon* into the little tape machine my sister and I owned, pressed the play button, then placed my headphones over my ears. It was evening, bedtime not too distant. I lay back and shut my eyes.

Only a few months had passed since I'd suddenly got into rock music. Most likely, that was the hormones, changing my whole perception of the world. But this album was somehow different from all the music I'd heard before. There was a track at the end of side one which moved me in a way I'd never been moved before. It somehow spoke – without using words – of the profundities of the human condition, of those great questions we all have to wrestle with, and, in the end, find an answer for. It evoked depths, distance, transcendence. I'd never heard anything like it. *The Great Gig In The Sky* stirred an emotional response in me for the first time. Even the mighty Tangerine Dream had not done that.

When I mentioned it to my parents the next day, my father, with all the sarcasm and mockery he reserved for his pronouncements on music, asked: "Did it send you then?" He used the terminology appropriate to his generation. Did it move you?

Yes, it did.

This was the beginning of my love for the music of Pink Floyd. I can visualise the moment with clarity. I don't forget moments like that. Music lovers never do.

That was 1977, and soon enough, I'd discovered that this was not a new band. They had been making albums since 1967, but those early offerings were different – weirdly different – to the smooth, spacious and synth-inflected music of the 1973 album. Their debut release sounded nothing like their most recent. That was confusing. As I went back in time to the 1960s then forward to *Animals,* which I heard for the first time on Annie

Nightingale's radio show, I realised this was a band like no other. Their music changed, progressed and expanded, just like the music of my other main love, Tangerine Dream. The Floyd were amazing! This was a group I wanted to be a fan of, just like Edgar Froese had been.

Four years later I found myself at university in a leafy suburb of Greater London. Pink Floyd were going to play *The Wall* live at Earls Court in June, and a girl student was advertising a couple of tickets for sale. I bought one, and went along. That was amazing too. Unforgettable, in fact. I bought the sweatshirt, of course, a white garment in cotton. It was a terrible fit.

Now, forty-three years later, with Pink Floyd missing Richard Wright and Syd Barrett, and no original members left in "Tangerine Dream," I find myself about to make a long journey, a journey in music, from the melodious whimsy of *The Piper At The Gates Of Dawn* to the elegiac dream of *The Endless Journey*. Along the way I'm going to hear music forgotten, half-remembered, and recalled with intensity: the studio disc of *Ummagumma*, that song they did after Roger Waters left, with the rowing boat introduction, and the sublime *Echoes*. I'm going to write about all those albums: the tracks and songs, their background, the group's influences, but most of all the effects of the music the albums contain on the human mind. For we are all people of music, whether we know it or not.

Music touches us. It moves us all.

Why Albums?

Younger folk listening to music these days have a problem. Or, at least, they do according to older folk.

I am one of those older people. My love of music – progressive, rock and electronic in particular – began in around 1977 when I was fifteen and at school. In those days, the preeminent musical forms were the single and the album. I liked songs released as singles, and I watched *Top Of The Pops* as often as my parents would allow, but the format that really spoke to me was the LP: the long-player. There was a natural beauty of form to the LP that spoke of the ideal design. It was the musical equivalent of the wheel, the book, or the teapot. Once invented, it was a fixture. Moreover, at twenty minutes per side, the LP enclosed the average human attention span to perfection. Chance brought it into being, and, once it had appeared, it began to be exploited by groups and artists with creative vision. The Beatles, of course, were the first to make a virtue of the simultaneous compactness and expansive possibilities of the LP, and not just with *Sergeant Pepper's Lonely Hearts Club Band*, which is not difficult to argue as the origin point of everything that followed. Their attitude of taking time in the studio to craft music became a standard methodology.

My first musical love back in 1977 was Tangerine Dream, but I soon discovered ELP, Yes, Genesis and King Crimson. And, of course, Pink Floyd.

I am a musician, a songwriter and a producer myself. I can say now that I have had no commercial success whatsoever. This brings many important advantages, the main one being that I was, and still am, able to record and release any album I like. One of my friends, pondering why my attitude to music was different to that of her acquaintances, described me as "a music builder." I was flattered by this, and it made me think about the stature and cultural relevance of the LP as a classic music format. All those musical works which for me have meaning and significance are albums of roughly forty minutes; not just prog or Berlin School, but punk, synth-pop and so on. The LP, crafted in recording studios, made with love and insight, with musicality and care, is endlessly fascinating to me. I never tire of discovering new ones.

All the albums of my own of which I am most happy were *built*. They were constructed, from musical building blocks, in my studio, often over long periods of time, with care and passion, with insight, effort and diligence. I have worked hard and thought long about the inspiration afforded by David Bowie in his maxim – and here I paraphrase – that the best place for an artist to be is just outside their comfort zone. One of the reasons that the early Tangerine Dream LPs on Virgin Records were so remarkable was that recording them was a considerable effort. *Phaedra* was not easy to make.

Bowie's maxim also applies to listening. Meaningful listening takes effort. It's not just a matter of choosing something then pasting it up all over the place like wallpaper. One of the tragedies of the internet is that, because of its vast size and its structure, it removes too much effort from personal life. It's easy. Too easy. Living life without making an effort is by definition easy, but easy is not necessarily meaningful; in fact, it rarely is. A life of little effort strips people of one of the foundations of their existence. Effort brings personal coherence, it brings satisfaction, it brings identity and belonging. One of the most notable consequences of our modern dependence on the internet is that our lives lack coherence, are unsatisfactory, reduce our identity to matters of race, creed or religion, and take all sense of belonging away. The so-called lonely crowd has become a lonely species. To be fair, a lot of these problems devolve from our insistence on following the capitalist, technocratic mindset, but the internet has made that problem far worse. And also to be fair, not all music is intended to be listened to in a meaningful way. That's fine.

In my view, the anonymous, antiseptic hands of the internet have touched music and spoiled it, and because of that, the way people listen to music has changed. Therefore, the significance and relevance of music to them has changed. This is a tragedy for humanity. It is a disaster. The notion of the album – curated by the artist or group, only by them, and set in stone for all time – is becoming a minority interest. My own attitude to albums appears to be dying.

The modern obsession with single tracks and playlists in a setting of near-infinite choice has robbed listeners of a profoundly satisfying experience, that of listening to one LP *as the artist or group made it*. A simple, even old-fashioned pleasure perhaps, especially the time needed to reflect afterwards. Quiet time. But I believe older listeners have the advantage here. Theirs is a musical world based on composed works, not on collections of individual songs. They have access to curated works, presented as the artists or groups intended. Not all music should be listened to like this, but some music, set in that context established during the 1960s and 1970s, is best heard as a whole. For context *matters*. Streaming offers no context of worth. It is an alienated experience, which, as such, has become the predominant mode of listening in our alienated times.

Music consisting of multiple streamed tracks becomes stripped of context, and therefore of meaning. It becomes sonic wallpaper. It is important to stress that this happens regardless of the genre of music or the skill of the artist. Wallpaper can be absolutely beautiful, but, even so, its purpose is to cover walls. The modern mode of listening, consisting in the main of lists of individual tracks, be they favourites, classics, new or cover versions, is to consume with diminished context; lacking meaning, lacking cultural context, without curation by the artist. Curating your own list is fine. It's the same principle as the mix tape on a cassette. But mix tapes existed for an extra purpose beyond the music. Sometimes, the music alone should take precedence. Why not listen to music as the artist intended?

Listening to the creative output of a group or an artist over forty minutes tells you something about that person or group. It is an act of connection from mind to mind. This is a valuable human experience. Of course, listeners don't necessarily want that all the time, but at least the possibility of enlightenment via the LP is present in that format. Listening to the streamed output of innumerable artists or groups tells you nothing about human minds, except via the lowest common denominator. Streaming is an experience of homogeneity: ersatz, insignificant.

This, to me, reveals the beauty of the LP as it was in the 1960s and 1970s. The artists and groups of that era wished to create something according to their creativity and their musicality. No matter if they were humble or sincere, or on the other hand that they considered themselves to be gods or geniuses. They, the artists, were the individuals in charge of preparing their LPs. The idea was that the listener could walk beside them for about forty minutes – or wander off elsewhere, as may be. You didn't have to buy their LP. But no listener devised their own walk, except album by album. I did not want to fragment my listening experience when I was in my teens. I wanted to discover what the artist or the group had to say to me over that forty-minute period. That *mattered* to me. And it still matters.

I view albums as gemstones of music. I want to experience the whole gem, as it is cut, as it is coloured, in the setting in which it is presented, as it feels to me. I don't want a jeweller throwing a bag of paste brooches at me.

Before Pink Floyd

There were a few groups extant before The Pink Floyd Sound appeared: The Screaming Abdabs, The Tea Set – and some before even those short-lived associations. Formed in 1965, the initial format was as a five-piece group, including Bob Klose on guitar. Klose was the lead guitarist of The Tea Set, and the unit did make some recordings, but Klose left before Pink and Floyd turned up, eventually finding a home in printmaking and photography. The early bands, frequently re-named, had featured Rick Wright on rhythm guitar and Roger Waters on guitar, but those instrument duties also got changed as the merry-go-round of pre-Floyd combinations continued. By the time the line-up was Barrett/Klose/Mason/Waters/Wright, only two names were in rotation: The Tea Set and The Pink Floyd Sound. When Klose departed in the summer of 1965, the classic quartet remained.

Roger Waters, Nick Mason and Richard Wright all knew each other from studying architecture in London, while Waters and Syd (Roger) Barrett had been childhood friends, with Waters, originally playing guitar, visiting Barrett's home to watch him strum and sing. As the early 1960s began to acquire colour in 1965, the proto-Pink Floyd was active in London, playing cover versions and extended sets with instrumental passages so that their paucity of songs was not a problem. But it turned out that Syd Barrett had a gift. With psychedelia imminent and all the hues of Swinging London appearing like spring flowers, The Pink Floyd Sound became known on the underground scene, exotic flowers of the counterculture with much promise and amazing light projections. Syd Barrett could not only write unique melodies, he had a way with words that echoed the lexical dexterity of Edward Lear, not to mention a vivid imagination akin to Lewis Carroll. His colourful imagination recalled the whimsy and logical play of Spike Milligan, then known in the main for his trailblazing Goon Show.

For it turned out that Barrett was also a trailblazer…

Chapter 1

The Piper At The Gates Of Dawn

For decades, *The Piper At The Gates Of Dawn* has occupied a space in my Top 10 Albums Of All Time list, only to vacate it if *The Dark Side Of The Moon* happens to stride in. I first heard it at school in the latter half of the 1970s, and recognised that it was somehow different from the Pink Floyd LPs I was more familiar with – the progressive group with awesome concepts. Yet, being so naïve and knowing little about music, I could not put my finger on *why* it sounded different. I just knew that it did, and I liked that differentness.

Now I know that this all-time great debut album is the sole Floydian child of Syd Barrett, who wrote almost every song and who in those early days was considered the group's presiding genius. And he was. But why? Who was this revered, remarkable man?

In a work about the group's albums, it is best perhaps to approach Barrett through his songs. Those songs exhibit a quality rare even then, almost sixty years ago, when quality melodies were two-a-penny and many bands had a presiding genius. How different from the pop music of today. Two gifts made Barrett stand out: his gift for melody and his gift for wordplay.

There are songwriters who have an instinctive flair for melody, and that gift often makes their work distinctive. For a few, whose gifts are so prodigious they dwarf even those of Syd Barrett, there are almost no peers – I think of Paul McCartney, Paul Simon, Burt Bacharach. Although Barrett was no Mozart, as is McCartney, he was quite the most extraordinary writer of melody, whose instinctive gift allowed him to pen melodies that rose and fell along half-unknown scales that even Macca would at first be baffled by. Only Barrett could write the tune to *The Scarecrow,* for instance, or his oft-quoted miracle of melody, *Bike.* Where melody comes from is a little-explored conundrum, but in Barrett's case, it came from some combination of his mind – perhaps his links to his own childhood and the nursery rhymes which resided there – and his musicality. His use of melody was part of his vehicle of communication, which also included the lyrics and the mood of his songs. Those moods, following psychedelic paths, ranged from whimsical through strange, all the way to profound. Yet even the profound songs were set in a landscape that owed a lot to the aura of childhood.

For Barrett, children's books were entrancing; not just an escape, but an evocation of a time in his life that he wished to re-experience when he was older. But that entrancing aura was not just about the delights of childhood, it was about the English landscape too. Barrett felt an instinctive union with the world of Kenneth Graham's *The Wind In The Willows,* which has a chapter in it entitled 'Piper At The Gates Of Dawn.' That chapter is an evocation of Ratty and Mole finding their pagan lord Pan, whose demesne in this book is the classic English landscape. The adventures of Ratty, Mole, Badger and Toad of Toad Hall spoke to Barrett in a way so many British readers of that wonderful book recognise; its love of nature, its descriptions of river and woods, its narrative simplicity, its evocation of an England yet to be harrowed by the many hells of the First World War. The golden light of summer illuminated Barrett's mind as he wrote songs about scarecrows and gnomes. Indeed, in the latter case, he was influenced by another children's classic, *The Little Grey Men* by 'BB.' This author was in fact the illustrator of the book, Denys Watkins-Pitchford, a man also in love with the English landscape.

The Little Grey Men is a delightful book – one of Barrett's favourites. In it, three gnomes living in the hollowed-out bottom of a tree decide to journey upriver in search of their missing friend. The book is filled with lovingly crafted descriptions of the English landscape, including elements that would be recognised by such painters as John Constable. The three gnomes have to survive off the land, fishing, hiding from big folk like you and me (no gnome must ever be seen by a human being), and distilling country wine – a task mentioned by Barrett in one of his songs. As an evocation of an English landscape now largely lost, it is hard to beat, and in many respects is not a children's book at all, except in that children can enjoy it just as much as adults. Perhaps adults grasp more of the context and deeper meaning. But none of the beautiful simplicities of this classic novel would have been lost on Barrett, least of all the uncomplicated, emotionally satisfying task of surviving without the need to do a 9-5 job, to be dependent on others, or to leave and lose a radiantly beautiful landscape. The worldview of both children's novels suffuses the album that Barrett and his three bandmates recorded. There were other influences, of course, including psychedelia and space travel, but that child's perspective and that love of nature and landscape were at least as important.

Other influences were Hilaire Belloc and Edward Lear. Lear in particular tapped into that same, very English sense of humour that is both playful and absurdist, which Barrett also mined. For Lear, the emphasis was on happy nonsense, with plenty of imaginary creatures and individuals. There existed an eccentric English world of playing with language for its own sake – an almost musical play, with its emphasis on internal rhyming and alliteration – but which also had a kind of eccentric natural thinking, taking the oddness of English life and viewing the rural or natural lifestyle in particular through that lens. Much of this was down to the strict hierarchies manifesting in England as the class system. It is from this harsh social reality that the absurdist side of English humour comes, a humour attractive to John Lennon and Spike Milligan as much as to Barrett. English humourists observe the absurdity, the unspoken rules and the self-serving traditions of the upper classes and mock them through absurdism. This does apply to authoritarian social circumstances elsewhere, but, in humour, the English way has never been bettered. The strictness of the class system begat the absurdity of English humour. Barrett and his heroes of literature – Belloc, Graham, Lear and 'BB' – all mined the same deep source.

Many of Barrett's most quirky melodies also evoke childhood. It is hard to listen to the tune of, say, *Bike* or *The Scarecrow* without thinking of nursery rhymes. I say this as a huge compliment, for there is nothing wrong with nursery rhymes, and certainly not with a good melody. Experts on the human acquisition of language emphasise that period in a young child's life when their parents, especially their mother, use a sing-song, highly emphasised and strikingly melodic form of speech, which among experts is known as *motherese*. This form of speech has distinct advantages for a child learning to listen and to speak, since it emphasises the separate parts of which human speech is made – the syllables, the components. Motherese developed over tens, if not hundreds of thousands of years, its purpose to make the critical task of acquiring language easier for very young children. This is a near-universal phenomenon. There are almost no cultures without it. Motherese fades once a child has the basics of language and is able to automatically separate out the components of language from which words and sentences are composed. That Barrett's best melodies have this quality of motherese, with their deceptively simple scales and flourishes, is another indication of the mental territory he was mining. He was reaching back into his own childhood and extracting through melody all that was most valuable to him. That value became concentrated into forms most melodic and marvellous in the debut Pink Floyd album, beautiful songs, innocent songs, evocative songs. It was this unique gift that made people think he was the creative heart of the group; and, for a short time, he was.

Space and space travel were also concerns of the group and the debut LP, though minor ones. Space meant interplanetary exploration and the race to the Moon, at the time a mind-boggling development. By 1967, Soviet citizens and Americans had walked in space, and the Apollo mission tests were well underway. Public awareness of the Space Race was high, leading to all sorts of speculation. Until 1969, scientists were unsure what kind of surface texture Neil Armstrong would walk on. Those early days were influential to many artistes – writers, visual artists, film-makers and musicians. Barrett and Pink Floyd were quick to link their stage and light shows with awareness of space themes. Barrett's lyrics and song titles riffed on space excitement: *Interstellar Overdrive* and *Astronomy Domine*, albeit that the former cut was more of an abstract affair conveyed through his guitar than a specific reference via the music.

Barrett's guitar style was not unique at the time, however. In those early days of psychedelia, a group even more 'out there' than The Pink Floyd Sound was performing at underground clubs. AMM were the ultimate delight for avant-garde heads, whose guitarist Keith Rowe was infamous for such tricks as rolling ball bearings up and down the neck of his guitar in the pursuit of ever more extraordinary sounds. But all these influences – space, avant garde music and bands, and literary influences – were not the goal for Barrett, nor for the men who managed and assisted the group. Though the group rejected the tag psychedelic pop, Barrett was not aiming for AMM-style esoteric music. His group were going to write *songs*, using his various influences as appropriate. Peter Jenner in particular did not want Pink Floyd to be lumped in with the various blues and faux-blues bands dominating the scene, not least because most of those influences came from America. What attracted him to Pink Floyd was their willingness to take popular tropes and whack them into unknown, where lay more interesting territory. They were freaky, they embraced electronic and avant-garde music, they were far out.

This is not to say that those classic English blues groups did not influence the four young men watching, nor the British bands then rising high. All of them were impressed by Cream – especially the volume that the band played at – while bands such as The Who and Cream convinced Nick Mason that he should ditch his studies and return to playing drums.

By autumn 1966, the group – still known as The Pink Floyd Sound – were at the head of the psychedelic explosion, playing venues such as the All Saints Hall in Notting Hill Gate. Although Barrett had been converted to Jenner's scheme, Mason, Waters and Wright were not quite so ready to embrace the new direction. Their playing was still a little amateur. But as psychedelia expanded and the Summer of Love came into view, they all followed suit. Thus was the multicoloured die cast.

That roll of the die was noted by many, not least the fledgling paper *International Times*. Though at first a little sniffy about the group's position in the burgeoning underground – too much pop and not enough freak – they soon became more supportive, and in doing so helped fix the tag psychedelic to the group. By then, the group was the house band of the UFO Club, and fame and fortune were both just a step away. Yet this was a fast-changing scene. By spring 1967, the group's agent Andrew King felt sure enough of himself to distance Pink Floyd from psychedelia, and, in the vaguest, most hip terms, describe the group as something beyond slogans – a "total experience," as King put it.

But it was not just outer space that was being explored. In 1964, esteemed British SF author Michael Moorcock took over editorship of *New Worlds*, a British SF magazine, and after a few years, a new batch of authors arrived, many of them, like J.G. Ballard, more interested in exploring inner space. Amongst members of the Underground, this was often done with LSD, the drug of choice. Although banned in Britain since 1967, acid enthusiasts inspired by the American LSD guru Timothy Leary and by such British institutions as a London office of the World Psychedelic Centre made sure the right people could access the right drug. Besides, the ethical framework surrounding LSD was too awesome to ignore. LSD promised union with the universe, with a new spiritual – and nonreligious – dimension; a true shake-up of established values. And free-thinkers, drop-outs and students in strait-laced Britain *wanted* that shake-up.

Our word psychedelia comes from "soul, to show" – Psyche, delein, from the Greek. It is no accident that the acolytes of acid believed in the possibility of LSD somehow changing the way individuals, and then society, could think. It was all about revelation – showing and experiencing their true selves in relation to the universe.

The two years before the Summer of Love were in Britain a time of extraordinary transformation. From being a nation of rigid, almost tyrannical tradition and conservatism, suddenly there was longer hair on men, shorter skirts on women, and an atmosphere of bewildering change. This was, for many, the antithesis of conservatism, and they opposed it. But among students, not least those studying architecture in London, the time for exploration was now. They would do that through music and with LSD.

Syd Barrett was one such explorer. As his legend now states, he lost himself as a consequence. The debut Pink Floyd album references acid and space without making too much of the drugs, yet those drugs were crucial in establishing Barrett's mindset as he composed more songs.

LSD arrived in Cambridge in 1965 via one Nigel Lesmoir-Gordon, smoker of weed and imbiber of the morning glory seed. LSD was then hardly known – and legal. The psychoanalyst R.D. Laing was an early proselytiser of its benefits, and soon became a well-known figure at underground events; he was, in effect, part of the counterculture. His books had a considerable impact. When Barrett was struggling with the consequences of his LSD intake, Roger Waters, knowing of Laing's reputation, tried to arrange meetings between the two, but on the first occasion, when the pair arrived at Laing's flat, Barrett would not or could not get out of their vehicle, and the second time, he would not even leave his flat. All Waters' efforts were to no avail.

Lesmoir-Gordon lived in Cromwell Road. Soon, he was an evangelist for the acid experience of universal love and union, and many of the residents of the flats where he resided, including Barrett, were LSD converts. Liquid

LSD would be dropped onto sugar cubes, then consumed. Vast quantities would be consumed without thinking of the possible consequences. Often Lesmoir-Gordon would return to Cambridge to try to "turn on," as the initiates had it, other people to this amazing experience, and soon he would in some circles be referred to as the Acid King. His flat at Number 101 became an "acid ashram," where he would guide novices through their first experiences. Other noted musicians of the time, including Paul McCartney, who stunned the nation when, much later, he confessed to acid use, and Donovan, knew and worked with Lesmoir-Gordon.

Lesmoir-Gordon filmed Barrett one day when Barrett was tripping in a quarry near Cambridge, a film later (and inaccurately) labelled *Syd's First Trip.* The drug was opening minds and flinging wide the doors of perception. Its adherents believed it could do no wrong. But it could, and it did.

As 1965 turned into 1966, The Pink Floyd Sound, now one of the groups attached to Hoppy Hopkins' Spontaneous Underground events at the Marquee Club in Wardour Street, became associated with acid, freaks, heads, and all things trippy. They were becoming the voice of the LSD movement and all the multi-coloured imagery that went with it, not least on the posters for their 13 March appearance. Buzz words recognisable by freaks and heads were everywhere: stoned, space-age, trip, astral, incense, far out… With The Pink Floyd Sound developing their novel light shows at the same time, and with many in the audience personally knowing the bands playing, the hitherto small acid scene was set to explode. By the time 1966 was underway and London was becoming Swinging London, media interest was sparked, the police were sniffing around, and things were beginning to get out of control. But at the UFO Club, Middle Earth and other haunts, acid was still available.

On 29 April 1967, at Alexandra Palace, an event of legend took place – the 14 Hour Technicolour Dream. This event above all others of the time was a public spectacle, where John Lennon wandered around, two dozen bands on two stages played through the night, and, at dawn, Pink Floyd – now managed by the man who would aid their formative experiences, Peter Jenner – played a set illuminated by the light of dawn streaming through the venue's windows. For Jenner, high on acid, as was Barrett, the event was a peak psychedelic experience.

Syd Barrett simply took more LSD than his brain could manage. As the golden light of the Summer of Love and Pink Psychedelic Floyd retreated when a new winter began, he was struggling with mental instability. The group was having to cover up for his wayward behaviour. Eventually, he was let go. None of the other members of the group were into smoking dope or dropping acid, though Jenner was always enthusiastic. Roger Waters, by contrast, was suspicious of Jenner's dope smoking. But, in the end, everybody moved on.

One final change in music culture brought about by *The Piper At The Gates Of Dawn* was the accent Syd Barrett sang with. That was British, not American. Interviewed in 1990, David Bowie remarked that, along with Anthony Newley, Barrett was the first musician he had heard singing with a true British accent. Before then, Americans had ruled the airwaves. This was yet another aspect of the glamour of Barrett. Bowie recalled seeing Barrett take charge of the stage, remembered Barrett's self-adornment and image, as well as being amazed by the creative virtuosity of the songs. It is indicative of the glamour of the man that somebody like David Bowie should feel inspired. Barrett's voice took on a timbre at times almost essence-of-English, not specific to any region but with diction and mannerisms that evoked the heart of England. You can hear it in his vocals for *The Gnome* and *Flaming*.

Pink Floyd released two singles before the August 1967 arrival of the LP. Both of them were quirky songs in English psychedelic mode, the first about underwear theft, the second set around the 'Games For May' event organised by Andrew King and Peter Jenner, then managers of the group. Both emphasised Barrett's lyrical skill, and had memorable melodies, the former with an unusual chord sequence too.

The opening track of the LP, however, thrust the group into space. *Astronomy Domine* began with the weirdest of weird voices (provided by Jenner), something most pop lovers would never before have heard on their transistor radios, a voice intoning some kind of space liturgy. But then the song hurtled into another dramatic chord sequence and part-hushed, part-ecstatic vocals that had nothing to do with doomed love, teen romance, or other concerns. These were impressionistic, poetic, even cut-up style lyrics, with a list of planets and a list of Shakespearean characters bubbling up halfway through. Except for the group and its acolytes, this music and lyrics came out of the blue. Almost nothing like them had been heard by British pop and rock lovers, especially the anthemic *woo-wooh-wooh* section. The guitar sounds, too, were bathed in reverb and delay, with a cutting intensity that sounded rare and novel. It was a new sound for a new era.

Lucifer Sam followed to bring the mood back to whimsy, its lyrics celebrating Syd's inexplicable cat. Anybody who has lived with a cat knows that explaining them is a pointless task – cats are meant to be experienced, not understood. Although Barrett's lyrics are rather cryptic, there is an element of this instinctive understanding of the true nature of cats in them. This song in particular utilises the multi-rhythmic lyrical style favoured by Barrett, in which he makes double or even triple rhymes in the same line: *Be a hip cat, be a ship's cat… hiding around on the ground…* The musical style was comparatively straightforward, with a loping, looping guitar riff and clattering drumming. The tempo was fast, bucking the groove here and there.

Matilda Mother spoke from the child's viewpoint. One of the most Barrett-esque of Syd's whimsies, its musical style was almost progressive, with various changes in mood and tempo. Rick Wright sang the verse, telling children's fairy stories of kings and silver, of bells and streams and wooden shoes, while Barrett, explicitly from the child's view, lamented how fairy stories had sustained him. There was a distinct sense of loss, even abandonment, in this lyric, and it is hard not to discern the same melancholy for a lost golden childhood that Barrett sensed in *The Wind In The Willows* and *The Little Grey Men*. The music had a way of weaving, of meandering even, with mournful keyboard solos that floated by just like clouds of sunlight. It was the perfect melding of lyric and music.

Flaming featured one of Barrett's most remarkable melodies, a confection of unexpected intervals and chords which resolved into a second melodic flight. The lyrics featured more fairy story fare, with unicorns, clouds, eiderdowns and various flowers of the field all included. But there was room in this surrealistic whimsy for a little technological development, with the immortal line, *travelling by telephone.* Only Barrett or Spike Milligan could have written that. Again, the music supported these whimsical odes to childhood, with tinkling percussion, use of short-period delay via tape machines, and the kind of keyboard sounds only Wright could wrest from his set-up. One moment of inspired genius was the cuckoo sound used to echo and mimic two notes sung by Barrett. The instrumental section, meanwhile, evoked rising into a multi-coloured sky like no other song, and it became the template for many later explorations of this peculiarly English style of psychedelia. Mason's drums were particularly important here, but the whole group coalesced to make this a classic amongst classics. Various live versions (for instance, those in *The Broadcast Collection* set) showed the group's attachment to this piece.

Pow R. Toc H. was a joint composition following the four Barrett solo works. Mostly instrumental, it used a series of groundbreaking effects and vocal techniques that even The Beatles were only just discovering. The mood is extraordinarily odd, with melodic whoops and ululations taking the place of lyrics; yet the melody these vocalisations follow is instantly memorable. Moreover, the emotional impact of the song is quite clear, as it moves from soft and jazzy to intense and half mad. The whoops become more like animal calls, and the music assumes an ominous new timbre, with a novel descending chord sequence. Nothing like this had ever been heard by rock music aficionados upon the LP's release. The group, Barrett in particular, were "out there" on their own. They found the path. They forged the template. They explored the undergrowth. *The Piper At The Gates Of Dawn* was their communique back to the rest of humanity listening, slack-jawed, on Radio 1.

A Roger Waters composition closed side 1, *Take Up Thy Stethoscope And Walk,* which was much more traditional pop-rock in style, though it did feature more strange vocal effects. This cut sounded like the group's freakout track, with a scything guitar sound that cut through everything, and a jazz-inflected keyboard solo from Wright. Its fast tempo and rock convolutions made it a brilliant closer to side 1 of the LP. The sneering style assumed by Waters for his debut vocal matched the acerbic lyrics criticising the medical profession.

Side 2 of the LP opened with another track whose influence has outweighed many others in the group's canon. *Interstellar Overdrive* became the ur-track for all space rock jams, beginning with Hawkwind, moving on to the more trippy Ozric Tentacles, and ending up with an ensemble of modern space rock outfits from The Spacious Mind to Litmus. The prototype had it all: it was instrumental, layered extended guitar solos and keyboard lines and effects over a solid backing, threw in a host of synthesized sounds, then headed off into orbit. This music evoked acid-enhanced space travel. Written by the whole group, it became a staple of the live act and was a fan favourite. The indeterminacy of the solos allowed creative flexibility and ensured the fans heard something different every time – always an advantage for a group pioneering long-form music. Barrett's guitar effects (legend has it that he invented the "gliss guitar" style of playing, in which a thin, polished object such as a Zippo lighter or the end of a screwdriver is brushed across a string or strings, resulting in an ethereal, drifting tone) emphasised the spaciness of this piece. Whatever the truth, his guitar sounds were mesmerising.

The closing drones of this lengthy ode to space segued straight into a song entirely unlike it: *The Gnome*. This song could be held up as the archetypal Barrett confection, in that it is whimsical, inspired by a childhood book, features a perfect, "nursery rhyme" melody of great beauty, and has lyrics which celebrate fantasy folk going about their daily business. This, as Barrett observed, included eating, sleeping, and drinking their wine. In a few minutes, it encapsulated everything that was unique about Barrett.

Chapter 24 also featured a beautiful melody, one of Barrett's top-tier tunes, but its subject matter was far more serious. Inspired by the twenty-fourth chapter of the Chinese book *I Ching*, it ran through the forms and consequences of the use of that book. In the mid-1960s, alternatives to Christianity, especially if they originated in the East, were becoming popular, and Barrett was no slouch when it came to such matters. It was another perfect song, so redolent of the era through its wide-eyed innocence.

The Scarecrow completed a trio of remarkable melodies, this one perhaps most suggestive of childhood songs and rhymes. It jumped up and down various scales in ways quite unlike anything else, before closing with a euphoric melodic twist. The music created by the group for this song emphasised mystery and delight, focusing on Wright's keyboard sound and softly clattering percussion, so that, with Barrett's most charming lyric about a scarecrow whose head did no thinking and whose arms did not move, the song was an LP highlight. The lyrics emphasised Barrett's wordplay within lines to great effect.

The concluding song on the LP has gone down in history as something entirely out of the ordinary, even for this group at this time. *Bike* was a delightful, trippy, surreal evocation of one man and his bike, the lyrics again full of intricate rhyming play, the music psychedelic to the maximum. It fell into two parts, the first telling of said man and bike, the second an evocation of a room of clockwork musical tunes into which Barrett invited the listener. What followed was a triumph of studio techniques. In 1967, the possibilities of weird sonic effects created by tape loops, double record and playback heads, and the like were beginning to be exploited, not least by Steve Reich, whose paean to looped tape effects and sonic disintegration, *Come Out,* was an early outlier of the possible. In Britain, The Beatles had utilised such ideas the year before for their trailblazing *Tomorrow Never Knows,* albeit with less feedback. For *Bike,* once the room of clockwork objects had been explored, a tape loop was prepared that sounded like a flock of electronic geese flying across London. Even today, this audio fragment sounds extraordinary. In 1967, it melted minds.

The artwork for the LP matched the refracted repetition of some of the group's lightshow effects. They wore groovy threads and emphasised colour. It was a typical ploy of the time, taking up that short-lived psychedelic baton as the Summer of Love reached its height, mimicking some of the effects of an LSD trip. By association, the group acquired a reputation for being messengers of the LSD revolution, including in the national press, but it was only Barrett who consumed the drug in significant quantities. Photographer Vic Singh photographed the group through a prism lens obtained from George Harrison, tripling the image of each of the four group members.

The music, lyrics, artwork and presentation of this debut LP were not its only extraordinary features. The location of the recording also had an impact on the group.

In 1967, Abbey Road Studios in London was the home of The Beatles, then bestriding the world like no other band before or after. Following the touring chaos of 1966, and with an unhappy George Harrison speaking up about burdensome events, the band decamped to Abbey Road, there to begin work on the transformation of the entire music recording process. In these precious months, they would lay the foundation for almost everything that followed in rock and pop music. Some critics eschew *Sgt. Pepper's Lonely Hearts Club Band* and head for *Revolver* as the greatest Beatles LP, but there is little doubt that *Revolver* was the culmination of what went before, whereas

Sgt. Pepper truly was revelatory, arriving unique and perfectly formed as if out of thin air. And it was while they recorded *Sgt. Pepper* and the double A-side single that preceded it that The Beatles found themselves sharing Abbey Road with a new group called Pink Floyd.

According to Nick Mason, the two bands did meet and mix. Mason recalls them all watching The Beatles recording the voice parts for *Lovely Rita*, which may have inspired similar vocal techniques and recording tricks for *Pow R. Toc H.* Paul McCartney was cagey, albeit with a knowing grin and a raised thumb, when through the early months of 1967 he was asked about the upcoming LP, but the members of Pink Floyd were next door at Abbey Road, and could not fail to assimilate some of the Fab 4's magic. But they too had a creative genius at work, Syd Barrett, and Barrett was receptive to anything that extended his musical range into the psychedelic wonderland he had in mind: *The Piper At The Gates Of Dawn.* Though at the time this LP had little of the world-shattering impact of *Sgt. Pepper,* it would in due course come to occupy a similar rank. The facilities, technical know-how and shared ambitions of the staff and managers at Abbey Road spread far and wide, The Beatles the main recipient, but Pink Floyd not much less. Some of that Abbey Road glamour threaded itself through the innocent wonder of *The Scarecrow* just as it did through *With A Little Help From My Friends.* In 1967, everything in popular music was up for grabs. Barrett and the group knew that.

Moreover, Paul McCartney in particular was interested in inhabiting that novel world between pop or rock music and electronics or the avant-garde, as evinced by the unique sound world of *Sgt. Pepper.* McCartney attended the *International Times* launch event, and even followed Pink Floyd into the UFO Club. He was intrigued by Barrett in particular, talking the group up in various pronouncements. What he liked about the group and the UFO was its quality of being more like a trippy play area than a music club. He liked the informality of it, the light projections, the freaky music – and the volume that music was played at. Pink Floyd were exemplars of that music and that counterculture attitude. They were spearheading a new sonic exploration. They were beyond groovy. They were *hip.*

When it came to recording music, the group's producer Norman Smith took on board McCartney's enthusiasm. He wanted to do more than sit behind the mixing desk performing standard duties. In addition, he wanted to be at the heart of the group. But that meant moving on from Joe Boyd's recordings at Sound Techniques Studios…

Until the mid-1990s, the earliest Pink Floyd recordings commercially available were those on the debut LP. But three decades later, a small, curious, yet far from insignificant release appeared. This was the *London '66-'67* EP, which comprised two tracks recorded for Peter Whitehead's film *Tonite Let's All Make Love In London*. The EP contained music which had been heard before by those in the know, but which had never appeared in any quantity or legal basis.

The first track was an extended version of *Interstellar Overdrive* – almost seventeen minutes of previously unreleased sonic journeying, with the group playing to maximum effect, sometimes psychedelic, but also dipping into jazz-inflected areas. The mix in the opening section emphasised Wright's keyboards – that unmistakable whirring organ sound – which then headed off into a meandering solo part. There was a lot of space here, nothing heavy, with the guitar part and effects loose and easy. As Barrett added clicks and clattering to his arsenal of electric sounds, the focus turned to his guitar. Meanwhile, the rest of the group stopped and started proceedings, alternately light and rocking out – a lot of chopping and changing from spacious to rock. It was the middle section of the LP version which was most extended, as various organ and keyboard solos vied with Barrett's psychedelic guitar.

At the time, this new version was a surprise, since the sheer weight of the group's achievements, especially in the 1970s, tended to overshadow the formative material. But a seventeen-minute version of *Interstellar Overdrive* not presented on a crackly bootleg LP was quite something in the era before our own, in which classic albums are regularly demystified by a process of evisceration and smearing over increasingly capacious audio formats. The sheer excitement of this kind of music being conceived, explored and played by visionary musicians is conveyed par excellence by this version, which trips and travels along various psychedelic avenues. It shows how adventurous the group allowed themselves to be. They really were ahead of the curve. They reflected in music and via their light-shows the true nature of the social changes occurring in Swinging London at that time: colourful, intense, transformational.

Equally good was the second track, which to all intents and purposes was "brand new." *Nick's Boogie*, composed by the man himself, was a bit rampant, a bit loose 'n' easy, but a delight to hear. A shuffling tom-tom beat opened proceedings, with bass and then guitar effects coming in, emphasised by Barrett's use of the Binson Echorec, an early delay unit using ferromagnetic tape. As Mason brought in a new beat and some cymbal work, the piece developed into something not a million miles away from the first track, but with its own ambience and charm. Weird guitar tickings vied with spacey keyboards, with the ending a slow power-down provided by Mason's tom-toms and another feedback loop on the delay tape unit.

As with the first track, *Nick's Boogie* was recorded at the Sound Techniques Studio in London during January 1967, the music produced by Joe Boyd. Later recordings may have been tightened up for the debut LP, but these looser, more experimental versions easily hold their own with the classic music. Their real value, though, is in showing how the group's music developed from a burgeoning, often jazz-based experimental music – *avant-garde* as it was best known at the time – in which formal strictures were thrown out of the window.

The modern reputation of *The Piper At The Gates Of Dawn* is deserved, but there is no doubt that the tragedy of Syd Barrett, falling into a pit of acid damage, increases its perceived value. So many musicians and groups have been influenced by the man: by his songs, his charisma, his creativity. Some musicians want to be like him – to be *him*. They want that mystical aura to surround themselves. Yet much of Barrett's glamour resides in just eight songs on the debut LP, two singles, and the later solo work, which, even through rose-tinted glasses, does not quite match the wonder of the Pink Floyd songs. It is a small canon. That brevity, a flame burning so bright but for such a short time, is part of the foundation of the legend of Syd Barrett. For those musicians who want so much to be him, it is probably for the best that they cannot repeat the events of the mid-1960s.

Syd Barrett was a one-off. We will never see his like again. But, though his legacy is small in quantity, the quality of the inspiration it can create is still great. To this day, sixty years later, that legacy is strong. It shows no sign of diminishing.

Chapter 2

A Saucerful Of Secrets

Syd Barrett and LSD went back some way. Even in 1967, as the group were finishing up recording sessions for the debut LP with Norman Smith at Abbey Road, Barrett had experimented with acid for some time, using his experiences and revelations to inform his songwriting. By the time of the album's release, Barrett's use was increasing. The potential side effects of tripping were known – the so-called bad trip – but the long-term damage that could be wreaked by this heaviest of drugs was as yet little understood. LSD had only been around for a few decades, and had only recently been banned in Britain.

When it came to touring and album promotion, the increasingly unresponsive Barrett began to struggle. His former full use of the stage diminished to reluctant appearances, when sometimes he would do nothing at all, arms limp at his sides. By the end of the year, he was in real trouble. Explaining to the media that Barrett was suffering from nervous exhaustion, the group and their managers tried to coax out the formerly charismatic, gregarious and popular Barrett from the atrophied figure they found themselves with, but nothing worked. Syd Barrett was disappearing into himself. He was smothering in acid-soaked damage.

Riding high on critical and commercial success, the group began to consider their next move. There were songs to be written, recordings to be made, but the matter of Barrett and his mental state was becoming impossible to deal with. With all this in mind, the group in December called upon the services of somebody already known to them.

David Gilmour had known Barrett and Roger Waters since their school days, and had met and enjoyed time with Barrett and others in France, and elsewhere. A strong, fluid and experienced guitarist, he was brought into the group to cover for the wayward and sometimes truculent Barrett. The idea was to keep Barrett on as a songwriter – clearly, he was the main source of music and lyrics – while the rest of the group played live and undertook all the other music biz tasks. Yet this did not work. With Peter Jenner and Andrew King leaving Pink Floyd because they considered Barrett to be the heart of the group, there was crisis and uncertainty afoot. But Gilmour was at least a known quantity, an inventive and lyrical guitarist, with long-term social links to Waters and Barrett. He was the group's best bet.

When it came to preparing songs for the second LP, Barrett in the end could only manage one, although others written around that time did appear on his solo work, including the song *Vegetable Man*. Wright contributed two of his very best, Waters also wrote songs, while the band also created other lengthy works, one of which became the new album's title track.

The LP opened with an up-tempo riff echoing some of the spacey moments of the debut, accompanied by crisp cymbal work from Mason. *Let There Be More Light* was a Waters composition with verses sung by Wright, his more delicate singing voice contrasting with Barrett's confident vocals the year before. Wright, however, caught the vibe of the song perfectly. Gilmour's stronger, more earthy voice sang the chorus, the pairing complementing and contrasting with one another to great effect. With the singing over, it was time for Gilmour to lay down his first-ever Floyd guitar solo, a slow, bluesy evocation of something mystical ascending into the sky. The song was a fine opener and became a staple of the group's live set for a few years. While there were echoes of the timbres of the debut LP, this song had none of Barrett's whimsy, hinting at some of the darker, more trance-like evocations that the group would explore as the 1960s passed by.

Remember A Day showed what a superb songwriter Richard Wright was. In melody, music, lyrics and feel, the song was a gorgeous evocation of nostalgia, with more than a hint of childhood lives, as with Barrett's own songs. Yet it was no copy, nor even an homage; it was its own creation, its lyrics recalling youthful exploits, childhood dreams, of days so long their evenings would seem never to arrive. Conveyed in Wright's soft voice, which by itself evoked the past, it threw the listener into reflections on their own childhoods, playing in gardens, climbing trees, pondering the sun… living a life free of concerns except play and exploration. This was a wholesome nostalgia, a theme Wright would return to.

Set The Controls For The Heart Of The Sun became emblematic of this developing new Pink Floyd, a firm live favourite with its possibilities for improvisation, a mystical trance of a song, half sung, half whispered, as if in fear of the interplanetary agents which might soon arrive. With the addition of unusual instruments like the vibraphone, it was a marvellous drift through spacey territory, Mason using timpani to evoke the polyrhythmic flight. For this recording, Syd Barrett was in attendance, his guitar in the mix alongside Gilmour's.

The third Waters song on the A-side was the first in what would be a long line of works on the theme of war. *Corporal Clegg* was a fairly traditional rock song, sung by Gilmour with the addition of various strange vocalisations, its melody memorable if not complex. The lyrics were to the point, poking fun at the military way; not exactly sarcastic, but not complimentary either. With harmonised vocals and a rich mix of sounds, its music carried Waters' direct lyrics well, concluding this side of the LP in style, a paper-and-comb solo vying with explosions and other war noise at the chaotic end. 1968 was a dark sequel to the bright and colourful Summer of Love, and this song, while not intended to capture the mood of the year, certainly matched violent times. It was a comment on the psychological inanities of war, accompanied by Mrs Clegg's nice drop of gin.

The title track occupied a large portion of the B-side. This bravura work of space rock developed themes declared by *Interstellar Overdrive* and, to a lesser extent, *Astronomy Domine,* opening with dense, formless sound, like the steel grey clouds before a thunderstorm. As more instruments entered the mix, the tone and emotional impact of the music began to increase, with new instruments, keyboards especially, creating new themes. At the climax of the first part, Mason began a rippling, thrumming drum line that supported the second part, with its whistling guitars, sonic stabs and weird oscillations. Pianos thrashed about while guitars popped and dived, the music evoking a storm of sorts, whether that was real or metaphysical. Pink Floyd were early denizens of this avant-garde territory – stylish and confident. The third section was the calm after the storm, its liturgical atmosphere conveyed by Wright's church organ sound, by the slow tempo, and by the addition of an angelic choir, mostly created by Wright, which took the track to its suitably heavenly conclusion. Although this piece did not match the songs elsewhere, it very much fitted on the album, providing a dense and intense pivot around which those other, more traditional songs rotated, with their terrestrial concerns of childhood, war and flight. It was a glimpse from space of the human intricacies of Planet Earth.

Wright's second song on the album was as delightful as his first, although it could have had a black heart. *See-Saw* was another evocation of childhood, this time revolving around a brother and a sister, living their young lives and going up and down on their see-saw. Of all the songs on the album not written by Barrett, this is perhaps the one which could have been, its gorgeous melody, impressionistic lyrics, concerns of children and childhood, and its subtle creation of nostalgia through images of the see-saw and the land in which it resides all merging to make something special. Yet some of the lyrics do suggest darker emotions: *laughter in his sleep, sister's throwing stones…* Many listeners viewed this brother-sister relationship as a difficult one, for all the soft backing vocals, relaxed tempo and intricate keyboard and mellotron work. The more this song is delved into, the more it reveals, despite the brevity of its images – essentially the see-saw, the protagonists, plastic and real flowers… and that hint of a black heart. Who knows? The listener interprets what they hear. Syd Barrett played the marvellous slide guitar that accompanied this song.

Now that Barrett was too ill to work to any extent, the transition between the group with him and without him was conveyed by the final song on the album: Barrett's goodbye. Its title, *Jugband Blues* (a jugband was an ensemble of folk or traditional musicians using mostly home-made instruments, including a jug), spoke nothing of the tragedy within. As Barrett sang one of his most idiosyncratic melodies, he referred to himself and appeared to be addressing the rest of the group. He told of a Syd not here – awfully considerate! – yet still writing the song. The lyrics pitted Milligan-esque logical impossibilities with images of a blue Moon and red garments. The chorus, however, managed again to reach an almost anthemic level, opposing the finely crafted verse of complex bafflement with a chorus of confidence, even hope. As the song began to conclude, there was a pause, then a final farewell from Barrett. Against a softly strummed acoustic guitar, he sang four lines layering enigma over deep questions. And what exactly is a joke? A dozen interpretations of that final line could be made, but surely he was referring to his experiences during the year and the previous one. He retained some insight into himself. In the end, he did know something of the disaster visited upon him by LSD.

The influence of the LP's title track would last for many years to come, inspiring bands in this and other genres. In the early 1970s, a new genre called space rock emerged, spearheaded by a band whose style and live shows especially would go down in legend through Britain's underground: Hawkwind. Founded by guitarist Dave Brock, Hawkwind developed a muscular brand of rock music emphasising space themes, unusual synthesiser sounds, and the kind of artwork that spoke both of inner and outer space. By the time the 1970s were underway, the group was creating albums, not least their iconic live album *Space Ritual*, which would gain fans for decades to come. Consumption of acid was a given.

The space rock genre developed over many years with *A Saucerful Of Secrets* remaining one of the templates, albeit with many variations. The other influential track from this LP on the space rock scene was *Set The Control For The Heart Of The Sun*. Uber-hippies The Magic Mushroom Band recorded a terrific cover version for their single *Magick Eye*. That brand of rock, with the emphasis on space themes and counterculture (especially drugs – the Free Festival scene in Britain was a keen promoter of various substances), grew in popularity as other groups merged progressive rock with space rock: Gong, Ozric Tentacles, The Spacious Mind, Litmus, Eloy, Nektar. What all of these disparate bands from different countries had in common was what Pink Floyd had encapsulated on that 1968 title track – the evocation of space travel, of hallucinatory interior travel, of extended instrumental passages. *A Saucerful Of Secrets* was a seed that led to many flowers, all of them colourful.

Fifty years after the release of this LP, Nick Mason put together a live group including long-time associate Guy Pratt in order to bring a little more exposure to the early songs, but also to emphasise the improvisational part of that era of the group. Nick Mason's Saucerful Of Secrets became for him an enjoyable, critically acclaimed and successful coda to his time with the group, which, as the 1970s passed by, became more of a stadium entity playing structured music. In 2018, Mason and his bandmates were more interested in sonic imperfection and things happening on the night. Saucerful Of Secrets became the perfect shorthand for that endeavour.

One of the instruments Richard Wright used in those early days was the Mellotron. Invented earlier in the decade, the Mellotron became an essential resource for keyboard players, an instrument which in due course would become the signature sound of certain groups and musicians, and which for some fans would epitomise progressive rock itself. The strings version of the Mellotron sound would perhaps be used best by King Crimson, though Genesis' Tony Banks was also a master. The choir Mellotron was used to extraordinary effect by Klaus Schulze, particularly on his masterpiece "X", while the flute Mellotron was Edgar Froese's favourite, used on a number of classic mid-1970s Tangerine Dream recordings.

The operating principles of the Mellotron were based on ferric tape. Each key on the keyboard triggered a tape of one note being played by the relevant recorded instrument – say, a flute. In effect, the tape cartridges inside the Mellotron were samples, analogue samples preserved on tape. Those samples had all been recorded in studios, then copied. Different mellotrons would have different sounds and timbres. When the choral sounds were used, an unearthly choir was summoned, delivering any chord the player desired; the same applied to other instruments, including brass, and even birdsong.

An early appearance of this distinctive, and now legendary sound was on *Nights In White Satin* by The Moody Blues, whose keyboard player, Mike Pinder, had just acquired a Mellotron in 1967. He was responsible for creating the fluttering riff that follows songwriter Justin Hayward's verse lines, thus turning a lovely song into a solid gold classic. Not too long before, The Beatles had used the Mellotron flute sound to open their psychedelic paean to Liverpool, *Strawberry Fields Forever*.

Wright used his Mellotron on the lengthy instrumental title track, albeit that its sound seeped into the mix. Those distinctively spacey sounds merged well with the guitar effects and pattering percussion, giving the middle section of the track its cosmic vibe. But the best use was on his gorgeous song *See-Saw*, where the strings Mellotron applied just the right keening sound to emphasise how the song dealt with childhood and memories of childhood. Even by itself, a strings Mellotron could make the listener *yearn* for something.

The position of Rick Wright in Pink Floyd has been likened to that of George Harrison in The Beatles, and there are similarities. Wright could be characterised as the Quiet One, for instance. After the delirious delights of the group's debut LP, he provided two outstanding songs for the follow-up and, especially in *A Saucerful Of Secrets,* acted as the magnetic focus of the music. His influence was subtle, even concealed, but for this album, it was present and of critical importance. This LP is somehow "of" Wright, a vibe that emanates from his signature keyboard sounds and through his great talent as a songwriter. Waters' three songs were good without doubt, but Wright's pair had glamour and the enigma of their melodies. They were more than just good.

In some ways, then, Wright was the heart of *A Saucerful Of Secrets* as Syd Barrett had been the heart of *The Piper At The Gates Of Dawn.* Though he later confessed to being more of a "jazzer" than a "rocker," he was there from the earliest days of the group, when psychedelia and rock merged. But when Pink Floyd were asked to record film soundtrack music, another group member showed his burgeoning skills.

Chapter 3

More

The film *More* was made by Floyd fan Barbet Schroeder as his directorial debut. Its soundtrack, their first music to be completed without Syd Barrett, was composed by Pink Floyd and released under the same name in the summer of 1969. By now, the group had parted ways with early producer Norman Smith, and both music and lyrics had to be prepared with haste during the winter of that year. Yet the group managed this with ease, using improvisation to flesh out basic ideas.

The film was very much of its time. Filmed mostly on the Mediterranean island of Ibiza, it concerned the lives of its two main characters, both drifters in a typically 1960s atmosphere of permissive society and easily available drugs, in their case heroin. It was not thought highly of at the time and received a few stinker reviews.

Why should this film – indeed, any film – need music to accompany it? Films are amongst our most immersive art and media experiences. Like myths, like legends, like books, like modern novels, whether read or listened to, they tell a story, something human beings have been doing for tens of thousands of years. With film, those stories are presented in ultra-vivid detail without the experiencer having to do very much. Some films do involve a bit of mental effort, but in the main, the work of narration is done for the audience. In 1969, when *More* was released, significant films included Stanley Kubrick's *2001*, Peter Fonda and Dennis Hopper's *Easy Rider*, *Midnight Cowboy*, *True Grit* and *On Her Majesty's Secret Service*. All of these films relied on music to aid their storytelling. But why?

The other thread connecting films with their audience is emotion. Almost all films have some sort of emotional punch. Most directors and screenwriters (like most authors) would emphasise that aspect of their art because emotions are at the heart of everything most valuable to us. Emotions are our way of conveying to one another in ways which cannot be missed all that is central to our experience of life: danger, frustration, joy, the possibilities of the future and the losses of the past. Emotions speak of social awkwardness, of ethical wrongdoing. They are filled with *significance,* something storytellers latch on to when they create their tales.

Barbet Schroeder's film did not at first require this support to emphasise its emotional content. The director's original idea was for the music to be part of the film's actual sound, in the way sound emerges from the speakers attached to a record player when that device is filmed. But the cult cachet of the group and the sheer quality of the five standout songs, all composed by Roger Waters and sung by David Gilmour, lent this soundtrack something more.

The LP opened with one of Pink Floyd's most gorgeous songs, *Cirrus Minor.* This track could be held up as the archetype of those pastoral, summery, acoustic songs which the group made such a success of for a couple of years. It began with a recording of birds in their natural setting, an evocation of nature, quietness, even of drifting dreams. After a while, a softly strummed acoustic guitar entered the mix, before Gilmour sang the descending melody that at once sticks in the listener's mind, and which, for me at least, is recalled at once whenever I hear birdsong of the same type. This beautiful melody cast a long shadow in the legend of the group. The lyrics pitted images of summer birds, warm meadows and gently rippling rivers against – in the final verse – more astral concerns: the Moon and the Sun. It was one of Waters' finest moments. Moreover, it concluded with one of the most haunting keyboard parts Wright ever committed to tape.

The Nile Song was just heavy. *Very* heavy. Its crashing guitars and punchy drums alongside Gilmour's raucous vocal gave it a most un-Floyd-like vibe, which to this day sounds a little odd when stacked up against what the group were doing at the time. It is, however, entirely a success at what it does. The music works as a piece, and the lyrics, with their emphasis on a mysterious golden-haired woman heading for "the islands in the sun," match that intense ambition. But the lyrics also emphasise a darker side, perhaps inspired by the narrative ploy of the use of heroin, with references to endless sleep and being dragged down; and "golden," as in *Golden Brown,* has been used since as a metaphor for the physiological effects of heroin.

Third up was *The Crying Game,* which can be heard playing on a transistor radio in the film. Slow, dreamy and mostly acoustic, it sounded like a real-time drift through sun-baked territory, with Gilmour's slide guitar solo towards the end doing little to break this evanescent mood. *Up The Khyber*, meanwhile, was the opposite – a joint Wright/Mason instrumental composition whose up-tempo rhythm and bass part thrummed with satisfying crackle, over which Wright laid piano stabs and a luxuriant keyboard solo.

Green Is The Colour was another of Waters' outstanding compositions, a song which soon became a live favourite. The yearning melody, sung with supple skill by Gilmour, matched its waterfall chord sequence and was instantly memorable. Another of the classic Pink Floyd pastoral numbers, it was a live staple for some time, and always much appreciated. The lyrics effortlessly evoked the experience of being on the island of Ibiza, with its references to blue skies and sunlight through white dresses, waves and hazy visions. This soundtrack version became, in due course, the full group version, with Gilmour offering up scat vocals to accompany his guitar solo during the outro.

The last of Waters' five brilliant songs for this film was called *Cymbaline*. Again featuring a memorable melody, it told of a cycle of delight and despair, of sheer drops and apprehension, of broken-winged butterflies and ravens, of ominous thunder. This was another of the songs that played through a transistor radio in the film rather than be used to underscore the action and dialogue. Both *Cymbaline* and *The Crying Game* are known to the film's characters: internal adjuncts. Side one of the LP ended with *Party Sequence*, a brief ramble through hand drums and an exotic flute.

The second side of the album opened with the film's *Main Theme*, which pivoted around a reworking of the bass part from *Let There Be More Light*. This cut had particularly hypnotic bass and drum parts, with Mason's tom-toms used to brilliant effect. It stood out on the album as one of the best examples of what, at the time, the group were beginning to develop, a way of writing music which lacked the structure of formal songs but which excelled through its fluid use of improvised parts. Wright's spacey keyboards were the perfect addition to this exciting rhythm track, with a slide guitar later on adding more sophistication to the mix.

Ibiza Bar was a reworking of the heavy style and music of *The Nile Song*, here slowed down a little for the chorus, which featured harmony vocals. *More Blues* was another somewhat incongruous Pink Floyd track, in essence a Gilmour-fronted blues recording with subtle underpinning from Mason and Waters. Deep reverb filled out the guitar sound, which situated itself at the heart of traditional blues territory.

Quicksilver was a return to the ultimate in space territory. Opening with gentle but strange sound effects, it mutated into novel keyboard parts accompanied by cymbals, then more spaced-out keyboards. As an impressionistic, floating wander through interplanetary paths, it was a triumph, impossible to hear now without reference to the early Tangerine Dream albums. Those LPs on the German label Ohr Records, to which Edgar Froese and his band signed around the time Pink Floyd were recording *More* at Pye Studios, were deft expansions on this fabulous track, influenced by the group's oeuvre via Froese, who had long been a fan. This track, though atypical of the film's soundtrack, was certainly typical of the great improvised music the four men were able to create.

A Spanish Piece, in contrast, was brief, its purpose to link the island of Ibiza to its Spanish heritage. An acoustic E/F chord strum provided the necessary Iberian input, with strange Spanglish words and vocalisations laid over the top. The LP closed with *Dramatic Theme,* in which another variant on the *Let There Be More Light* bass part was created, over which various keyboard and guitar parts were laid. In this recording, the group were just as successful as they were with *Main Theme.*

In 1968, ten years had gone by since the first commercially popular stereo recordings. Record companies had mostly stopped putting 'Stereo Sound' or '360 Sound' on their LP covers. The *More* soundtrack music made much use of stereo, panning various sounds and instruments from left to right and back again, in a way popular for a while but which in due course became rather old-fashioned, although careful placement in the stereo spectrum would always be part of the Pink Floyd way.

This album could easily have been a studio LP – the lauded and successful follow-up to *A Saucerful Of Secrets.* It had five superb compositions from Roger Waters, which by themselves carried the LP, and which, with the addition of *Quicksilver, Up The Khyber* and *The Nile Song,* made something memorable and attractive – none of those "difficult third album" problems that bedevil so many groups. Yet Peter Jenner and Andrew King, noting the fragmenting relationship between Syd Barrett and the rest of the group, threw in their lot with Barrett, parting ways with the band and setting them free of their Blackhill Enterprises foundation. Part of this was because Barrett was deemed the creative genius of the group – the one who provided almost all the songs. But the *More* soundtrack proved that Roger Waters could also write excellent material; and it was already known that Richard Wright could. Pink Floyd then, based on their third release, were still potent. Yet 1969, as it moved from spring to autumn, saw a problem arising in the group's encampment. That problem lay in a lack of direction and an unexpected paucity of new material for the LP that would become the group's third studio work.

There was trouble afoot.

Chapter 4

Ummagumma

How does a successful group deal with the loss of one of its main members? Even, the *main* member? For this, it seemed, was what Syd Barrett had been to Pink Floyd.

Some groups, such as The Stranglers, go on regardless. A few of us hardcore Stranglers fans did not follow them into post-Hugh Cornwell territory, but the remaining trio were happy to do so, while Cornwell went on to give us a terrific solo career. Some groups, like The Byrds, do likewise and more, as that band did after both Gene Clark and David Crosby departed. Genesis, Yes, Tangerine Dream and King Crimson all boasted various line-ups before their "classic" form emerged, in the case of Genesis, managing to sustain the quality of their music following the momentous loss of Peter Gabriel.

For Pink Floyd, now a quartet without Barrett and with David Gilmour, there was plenty of live work to be done, showcasing a collection of remarkable songs. But new music to be recorded in the studio was more problematic. It was a case of going from the sublime to the (nearly) ridiculous.

The live disk of the double LP *Ummagumma* (Cambridge slang for having sex) showed a group who had mastered their craft. Opening with *Astronomy Domine,* the stuttering keyboard sound created by Wright began a tight, controlled and euphoric sonic trip, with Waters playing exemplary bass and the harmonised vocals working to perfection. This was a version of the Barrett-dominated past that, if somewhat jarring in the context of *Ummagumma,* did illustrate how the group had survived his departure and accentuated their own skills and vision. Waters in particular came across as an energetic and inventive player. Gilmour, meanwhile, contributed a novel wah-wah guitar solo that somehow bridged the gap between Barrett's psychedelic sound and his own, more bluesy style. This opening section then segued into a lengthy, deep space sojourn founded on Wright's keyboards:

intricate, drifting, trippy. After the return of Waters' bass, more quiet drifting took place, before the return of the group and the full impulse of the main musical theme. Gilmour's slide guitar again seemed half Barrett half himself; wholly successful, however.

Careful With That Axe, Eugene was one of the group's live standards, played in multiple different versions. This version opened with a particularly light touch, Wright's subtle keyboard solos conveying a cosmic version of earlier styles. Alongside the lonely, meandering vocal, his organ sound had a hint of that used by Bo Hansson in his revered *Lord Of The Rings* LP, recorded during the same year as these live performances. This light touch emphasised the contrast afforded by the mad section to follow, with the screaming voice and Gilmour's effortlessly ascending guitar solo in sonic unison. And it really was crazy. Gilmour and Wright also worked well together, panned hard to the left and right sides of the stereo spectrum, with Gilmour's voice entering the mix as he began mimicking the notes he was playing. The concluding part stuttered as it fell out of the mix, leaving Wright to delight the audience with another cosmic keyboard breakdown. This was one of the finest versions of the song put to tape, deserving of its place on this live LP.

Set The Controls For The Heart Of The Sun was also here represented by some superb music, emphasising the spacey, expansive quality of the piece, supported to perfection by Mason's rippling and mesmeric percussion. Wright, meanwhile, used his "ultimate Wright" keyboard sound, which characterised this phase of the group and which gave him a central place in the sonic heart of the group. Waters' vocal was understated, even frail, echoing the vibe of the music. The main instrumental section also featured brilliant interplay between Wright and Mason, with Gilmour's wah-guitar adding texture. After a sudden halt, the music returned to its main riff, before a *really* spacey section brought Wright and Gilmour to the fore again. Concluding with a reworked version of the main riff, this performance – always a fan favourite – evoked the interstellar vibe of the group and remains without peer even after the post-copyright expiry release of other versions.

The live LP concluded with *A Saucerful Of Secrets*. A staple of the live shows since its inception, the piece was here given a calm, contemplative opening, with Wright and Gilmour both on fine form. The sudden crescendo and link into the second section allowed Mason to shine behind the drum kit, that hypnotic drum pattern, with its subtle allusion to *Tomorrow Never Knows,* underpinning an almost unhinged solo from Gilmour. This part evoked the kind of mystical visual experiences filmgoers seeing *2001* were reporting in the "Corridor of Light" sequence: relentless, vivid, intense. Pink Floyd, with their acid-inspired past, were the perfect group to make such connections between psychedelic experiences and music. Wright's heavenly keyboard sound made the bridge to the final section, with deep reverb and Gilmour's vocal both complementing each other. Gilmour's vocal here was rarely, if ever, bettered – impassioned and anthemic.

This was Pink Floyd showing that their chemistry and sonic imagination were more than just that provided by four individuals. With Wright and Gilmour's interplay, Waters' inspired compositions and bass, and Mason's drumming all coming together through the latter three pieces in particular, they were riding a wave of concert success that merited the release of a live LP at a comparatively early phase of their career. But *Ummagumma* was conceived as a double album. There was a studio half also.

Was it through frustrated irony that Richard Wright named his four-part suite *Sysyphus?* Perhaps, perhaps not. For Sisyphus was the figure in Ancient Greek legend who, once he had died of old age, found himself pushing a boulder up a hill, only for it to roll back down again, whereupon he had to repeat the task without cease. That meaningless, futile task could be hauled out as an analogy to describe the notion of each group member filling half a side of vinyl with music of their own conception: four solo spots on a group LP. But it was through such unwieldy concepts in later years that progressive rock acquired its reputation for pretentiousness.

Roger Waters had given five of his best songs for the *More* soundtrack, leaving his fuel tank almost empty. The other three members proffered instrumental pieces or half-decent songs. Forty minutes to fill…

Some fans would never describe the *Sysyphus* suite as meaningless and futile, but it certainly lacks charm, and is not exactly sonic manna from heaven. It has a quality about it as of hard work done with little reward: rock-smashing on a chain gang, perhaps, or cutting the grass in the local park. Opening with an introduction of mellotron and timpani, it moved into a musical theme of sorts, with a bold and brassy character. For the second part, Wright brought in his piano, playing an impressionistic solo that rolled up and down the keyboard, foreshadowing the kind of music Keith Jarrett would become famous for, except this was not as good. When more percussion entered the mix, Wright moved on to chunky atonal chords, which went a little crazy at the end. Overall, it was not bad music, just lacking in charisma. Part three of the suite featured percussion and more stolid piano chords, with the benefit of added sound effects. Weird voices gave the impression of sped-up tape being used, which in due course built to an audio climax. This section was mercifully brief. The final part began as a soft keyboard meditation with more mellotron, before birdsong and water recordings crept into the mix. Further keyboard effects and some drones moved the vibe to more of a *Saucerful Of Secrets* place, with a few guitar effects also, before the return of the demi-Crimson mellotron theme.

There is nothing repulsive or amateurish about this music. Rather, it lacks all Wright's customary charm, glamour and use of melody, which places it into the category of music the listener only ventures towards once. I cannot be certain, but I think the listening I undertook of the studio album before writing this chapter was my second one. I never bought the LP, though until recently I did own the CD. There will not be a third listening.

Roger Waters' half of side 1 came in two parts, one a piece better known for its title than for any musical quality: *Several Small Species Of Furry Animals Gathered Together In A Cave And Grooving With A Pict*. This audio collage was composed from five minutes of birdsong, weird voices and mouth noises, before various percussive effects entered the mix to provide the forward momentum of a rhythm. As I recall from my first listen all those years ago, it is amusing once. Voice tape loops then vied for attention with sped-up voices, before Waters assumed a Scottish accent and headed off into a kind of bizarre rant, a voice he would later use on *The Happiest Days Of Our Lives* from *The Wall*.

Yet *Grantchester Meadows* showed that his fuel tank was not entirely empty. This beautiful song matched the beautiful ones he had sunk into the *More* soundtrack. Birdsong on a tape loop introduced the listener to the song, with a softly strummed acoustic guitar signalling its beginning, in due course stating the melody too; and this melody was a gorgeous one, sustaining the entire song. As he sang his golden-hued lyrics, Waters evoked all the bucolic scenes the group would rely on for quite a few years, until the arrival of the heavyweight concept albums. Here were kingfishers and mist, the stirring of the day, larks and a dog fox. Here was pastoral comfort, English, in summertime. For the instrumental section, waterfowl and more birdsong recordings were employed to underpin the mood, with the final statement of the theme performed with harmony vocals. This was the finest song on the studio disk of the LP, and would for a while be played live, indicating its importance in the Floyd canon.

The second side of this LP was given over to Gilmour and Mason. Gilmour's *The Narrow Way* came in three parts, the first comprising a pair of acoustic guitars with a Balearic feel to them, over which guitar effects hovered. It was pleasant enough, with a nice slide guitar situated over the top, alongside a few backwards tape effects. The second part involved heavy riffing, with a hint of early Black Sabbath to it in the guitar timbre and vibe. Atonal keyboard and guitar effects surrounded this music, with an ambient section at the end as the riffing faded out. The third part was a song, one that the group even performed live now and again. With vocals sung over an ominous descending chord sequence, the strong tune and harmony vocal chorus made it the second-best track on the album. As the full band turned up to accompany Gilmour, momentum built nicely and there was a proper musical conclusion featuring twin guitars. But while not as charisma-free as Wright's effort, this was hardly Gilmour at his best.

Nick Mason offered the listener another multi-part composition, his *The Grand Vizier's Garden Party*. Part 1, *Entrance,* was performed by an uncredited Lindy Mason on flute – a brief flirtation before the main part, *Entertainment.* This comprised seven minutes of flailing around with drums, percussion and various strange keyboard and sound effects. There was plenty of audio thunder in the form of rolling timpani, which Mason did play with gusto. In due course, however, as the listener's eyelids drooped, a lonely keyboard sound emerged, softly reverberated and haunting, which too soon broke up into more random tape effects – then a bit of a kit drum solo. As with Wright's suite, this was not bad music, just unlistenable and pointless. *Exit,* part three of the extravaganza, brought the return of the flutes, this time multi-tracked.

So the studio LP was over. Finished. It could be placed back into its paper inner sleeve, never to be played again.

That the live disk of this album so outshone the studio disk was both a sign of the times and an indication of creative difficulties. To be fair, the group had devoted a lot of their most excellent 1969 material to the *More* LP, to that release's great advantage. Yet the dull corrosion of most of the *Ummagumma* studio side and its propensity to induce yawns did at least indicate a failure of vision. A live disk alone would probably, in retrospect, have been better.

But *Ummagumma* live did indicate that Pink Floyd, when summed, did not always add up to 4. It could be more – much more. Two of the four songs on the live disk were never released elsewhere in their time, and the live version of *A Saucerful Of Secrets* was outstanding. This was a group whose members could work to create synergy, whose musical chemistry was obvious, and who, given enough time, could compose music of great power and charm. The live album was, in fact, the main performance, with the studio disk an addendum for interested parties. Yet there would be no more live albums for decades.

Chapter 5

Zabriskie Point

Recorded in November and December 1969, the tracks that make up Pink Floyd's contribution to the film *Zabriskie Point* can be found in various combinations and in various orders on a number of albums. By this point in the year, the group had also recorded all of the *Ummagumma* LP.

The film epitomised the zeitgeist of the late 1960s. Directed by Michelangelo Antonioni, it portrayed the lives of two Americans, Daria, an anthropology student, helping a property developer who is building a village in the LA desert, and Michael, on the run for allegedly stealing an aeroplane, and perhaps for killing a cop in a riot. The film was part plot, part hazy depiction of America at the time, the sort of drifting narrative now called indulgent, then considered novel and exciting; a move away from the norm. Visually, it was stunning, with the silver screen used as if it were the canvas for a painting. In impressionistic drifts, it soared from scene to scene, a verité dream, a surrealistic pillow on which to rest the gaze.

Pink Floyd was not the only group involved in the soundtrack. The Grateful Dead were there, of course… and Jerry Garcia too, plus The Youngbloods, The Kaleidoscope, John Fahey and Patti Page. Yet Pink Floyd emerged as time went on as a major contributor to the vibe of the film, their music – part psychedelic, part ambient, with hints of progressive rock to come – adding to the dreamlike quality of the film.

In the intervening time between then and now, various alternate takes and unused recordings have been released, but the core tracks are constant. *Crumbling Land* was one of the most distinctive, a gorgeous, rolling, hippyish song featuring a lot of Gilmour: he sang, and played the clawhammer fingerpicked-style guitar accompaniment. The vocals were choral, with harmonies, so this came across as a summer tune from the tail end of the Summer of Love; and it rolled a beautiful melody. Summer was one of those identities the group took on following the loss of Syd Barrett, conveyed by Wright and Gilmour in particular, who both had the ability to write a lovely, lilting, summery tune.

Heart Beat, Pig Meat was a mash-up of various sources: something like a tribal rhythm, something like a spectral voice keening over the top of it, with various sound effects and stabs of other music and voices laid over the top. It was allusive, hallucinatory. The bass and Hammond organ gave it that Pink Floyd sheen, but something else seemed to be at the heart of it, a nod to European avant-garde perhaps, or American cut-up vendors. It was Pink Floyd, but uncomfortably so.

Country Song was a mix of Wright's piano and Gilmour's guitar, the latter played with a whammy bar. It weaved and walked along a musical ridge halfway between rock and un-rock. In *The Riot Scene,* meanwhile, there was just Wright's piano. The clawhammer guitar picking returned for *Unknown Song,* which in its latter parts featured drums and bass, and light keyboards too. This started off spacey and slow, giving the impression of being more of a jam than anything else, though Gilmour's guitar was never off-message. Already, he was refining sounds and styles for which in later years he would become famous. *Love Scene,* meanwhile, was a very slow blues, and *Red Queen Theme* another slow, summery song.

One of the recordings evoked a song for which the group would become famous. *Come In Number 51, Your Time Is Up* sounded a lot like *Careful With That Axe, Eugene.* Opening with soft, strange vocalisations and cosmic effects, the piece meandered artfully for some time before crashing into a much more intense section, with thrashing drums, octave bass, and a screeching, screaming voice: intensity to the maximum, heavy and bizarre.

Softness and intensity combined into one – a kind of psychedelic grunge decades before grunge – would be the touchstone for the album to follow, which, in terms of musical ambition, would blow the studio side of *Ummagumma* out of the water.

Chapter 6

Atom Heart Mother

tom. Heart. Mother. Even the album's title was fragmented, though it came from a newspaper headline noticed by chance. Atom Heart Mother in inky headline type on newsprint, three words related only through that chance association. This album title spoke of units merged into a whole, yet somehow only just transcending that association. There was only a hint of the union that would be obvious on later albums, although the *Atom Heart Mother Suite*, taking up the whole of the first side of the LP, was a pretty good try at group harmony. But Pink Floyd – that cult art band who used to have Syd Barrett – were still several species of musicians gathered together in a recording studio and grooving with an engineer. Although on this LP there was no overt separation into solo artists as with the studio disk of *Ummagumma*, the separation between each group member was clear. Three had a song of their own on the second side. The final psychedelic breakfast was also separated into individual sections, with the band coming together at the end. But those solo songs were good ones. Moreover, the huge piece of music that occupied side one was special; the most coherent large work that the group had composed for a while. It undoubtedly added up to more than 4.

Roger Waters would later badmouth *Atom Heart Mother*, mocking this early, primitive, experimental work from his elevated position as Provocateur General of Prog. In fact, it was a really good album, far better than *Ummagumma*, more coherent and a better listen than side one of *Meddle*, with a distinct move into grand ambition that hinted at triumphs to come.

The context of the album had also changed. With the Summer of Love a distant memory, the discomfort, aggression and fear of 1968 still potent, and the American space race win of 1969 fresh in everyone's minds, 1970 marked the last gasp of original psychedelia – the English variety in all its quirky whimsy, the American variety in its multicoloured intensity. 1970 marked the first stirrings in the nation's consciousness of progressive rock, although albums in that style had been released before, and during the first year of the new decade: *In The Court Of The Crimson King, The Yes Album, Trespass, Emerson Lake & Palmer.* All these works spoke of something new stirring amongst the nation's favourite rock bands, a move to complexity, to classical influences, to long-form work, and away from the 45 single format. Singles were for pop bands. These early LPs by groups soon to be labelled progressive rock were serious works, their vision expansive, their reach broad, their music sophisticated. Prog, after all, was a reaction against triteness, against the pop charts, even against the whimsy of psychedelia. Progressive rock was ambitious, grand and often visionary. It took majesty, complexity and sonic opulence from classical music, seethed it in recording studios rapidly changing from four-track to eight-track to sixteen-track, then floated lyrics far beyond pop concerns of love and heartbreak over the top. In some instances, over the top was where the music ended, but in 1970, only a collective gasp could be heard from the (mostly) young men who were getting into prog rock. There was no mention of pretension, bloating, bombast and pomposity. Not yet.

Pink Floyd had been progressive since 1968, but nobody had invented that category then. They sidestepped into prog by accident but also by inclination, manifesting the genre's core principles, yet only because they were heading roughly in that direction anyway. The *Atom Heart Mother Suite* featured a brass section and a choir; hardly the usual trappings of rock music, certainly not anything to do with quirky psychedelia. This was an expanded palette, eschewing guitar/bass/drums/vocals for something much more unusual. There were taped sound effects too. It was also a move away from American-inflected music based on blues, R&B and soul to something distinctively English, something pastoral, something orchestral, something far removed from girls, boys and cars, and girls and boys in cars. Psychedelia had originated on America's West Coast. Prog rock was an English movement, and as such, the four perfectly English men of Pink Floyd were a natural fit. They were understated, undemonstrative, scholarly and arty, and they had the right accents too. The England of 1970 was a class-based society with little to distinguish it from the class-ridden world of 1940, or even of 1910. And Pink Floyd were from the better echelons of the English pecking order.

Side one of the LP contained the *Atom Heart Mother Suite,* a long-form piece broken up into different musical sections. Opening with a throbbing keyboard chord, the piece gathered pace with various strange sounds and effects, before the main theme, stated by the brass section, began. And it was a really lovely theme, a fact overlooked by some critics in their zeal to scorn the piece. In fact, it's nearly an earworm – for this listener, at least. Once the theme was stated, a related theme began, played by a solo cello; also lovely. Already, this music established itself as melodic, beautifully arranged, subtly strange. There was a kind of exotic majesty about it, conveyed by the choice of instrumentation and the suppleness of the twin melodies. Mason's staccato drums picked a new rhythm out of the aether, complementing the cello while supporting it, as Wright's Hammond ostinatos added another layer. In the mind of the listener, some weird, nostalgic, velvet environment was evoked, somehow English yet strewn with luminous cushions from another world. It was neither overtly psychedelic nor avant-garde. It sat in an alternate world, close to the listener, at once familiar yet delivered by Morpheus. That alternate world was tangible also through the use of sound effects, all of them with a war theme: horses, guns, explosions. But they were brief, like the memory of a nightmare.

A new trip followed in which the choir was central. Opening with a haunting vocal refrain, the choir slowly built up, refrain by refrain, as the female voices were underpinned by male voices, until a marvellous unity of band and choir was achieved. This use of the human voice gave the piece – which otherwise might break apart into a collection of mere ideas – a delightful unity, the choir at once enfolding and delineating the piece. It was one of the most memorable of all the group's instrumental ploys, at once its own setting and evocative of similar vocal arrangements, for instance, that used by Stanley Kubrick in his just-released space epic *2001,* in which *Lux Aeterna* by Ligeti played a central role. Not that Pink Floyd's choir copied it; not at all. Yet for spaceheads of a certain type, the connection was clear. The group, after all, had on 20 July at the BBC TV Centre played live to accompany the Apollo 11 moon landing, a piece later named *Moonhead.*

From that glorious choral interlude leapt one of the group's best key changes, as a full band rock part began, floating a Gilmour guitar solo over a more traditional backing. It was in fact, a great solo, showing off Gilmour's string-bending technique whilst evoking a new, slinkier, more streamlined kind of space ride. In that solo, some of the seeds of later guitar triumphs were sown. After this part, the choir returned, this time with hypnotic effect, adding alien words of unknown origin and meaning to the mix, the vocal effects staccato, rolled, euphoric and enigmatic. Whatever it meant, it was effective to the highest degree. It took the great Tangerine Dream, and two years later, to record anything so startling, their track *Wahn* from the LP *Atem*. But, as often the case, Pink Floyd (whom Edgar Froese idolised) got there first.

From all this melodious tripping, there followed an eerie section founded mostly on sound effects, though with musical inserts. At the end, its climax concluded with the sound of a train approaching and passing at speed, something Tangerine Dream would also use later, halfway through their 1979 masterpiece *Force Majeure.* But this train, unlike the later one, would not take the listener into orchestrated synthesiser sequences; it took them into some kind of post-conflict landscape. This much more eerie place felt more like a deadly playground than anything more wholesome. The martial sound effects from earlier could now be recalled, their consequences obvious. And in the end: *Silence In The Studio!*

To finish the suite, the twin melodies returned, again stated on brass, with the choir and with the group, the tempo slowing down as the music reached its final, triumphant chord. The trip had been made, both in human terms via the choir, through uncharted space by the group, and yet all in English style. Soulfulness was elegance here, guitar histrionics restrained, albeit evocative, with the human voice never allowed to express much emotion. That choir was the entry point of the suite and much of the reason it worked so well, yet it also stood as the human interface of a musical experience more softly strange than any other. Those barked, rolled and half-shouted vocal fragments halfway through sounded like an alien communique, with the band, Mr Spock-like, raising one eyebrow in mild surprise at what they were experiencing. No American group could create so muscular a piece so wreathed in quiet mystery. This was classic Floyd. Of their peers, only Tangerine Dream and perhaps King Crimson could record anything akin.

A new factor in the recording of this album was the presence of a non-Floydian person. This was Ron Geesin, brought in to bring focus to music deemed by the group as missing some significant element. This he did while the group undertook an American tour, orchestrating the brass section and the choir into what in due course emerged as the heart of the final suite. There were obstacles. Abbey Road Studios had implemented a new eight-track machine with a high-tech mixer, stipulating that the era of making tape edits with razor blades was over. This meant that Mason and Waters had to play the entirety of the backing track in one go, leading to minor tempo issues later on. But, with the melodic aspect sorted and the vibe of the piece coming together, with Gilmour and Wright taking charge of various parts of the multi-section work, the *Atom Heart Mother Suite* was beginning to sound like a success. Geesin's input proved critical to the impact of the piece; his orchestrations, though difficult in places, giving majestic cohesion to it all.

Ummagumma had epitomised the group's lack of direction following the departure of Syd Barrett. The studio disk was a mess. While it surely underlined the group's cult status and their ability to consider unusual creative ideas, as two twenty-minute listening experiences, it was a bit like wading through treacle. Yet following the exotic, adventurous, but also musical, enjoyable and satisfying group composition on side one of *Atom Heart Mother* came another selection of solo works. How would they fare?

If was Roger Waters' contribution to the opening trio of songs on side two of the album. A lament for personal inadequacy and lack of empathy, it rolled along over a melancholy fingerpicked guitar in a style which in due course would become something of a trademark for Waters. But as yet, his tendency to lugubrious lament was only apparent through this song, his voice frail and with just enough wobble to convey emotional sincerity. But it was a well-fashioned song, its memorable melody capturing regret with some style. The lyrics were impactful enough to make the listener think, yet were neither overblown nor ill-judged. It was not the best song on the LP's second side, and perhaps should not have kicked it off, but all these decades later, it still packs a punch. Gilmour's guitar, meanwhile, alongside the softly incandescent keyboard part introduced by Wright, added to the dénouement of the song, bolstering its fragility with some good old-fashioned musical common sense — the sonic equivalent of an English-style pat on the back in lieu of anything more heartwarming. Yet the conclusion of the song was unexpected and swift enough to imply confusion and doubt once again. *If* was a first mature rendering of what over the rest of the decade would amount to Waters' new, clear and distinct direction for the group. There would be no more grooving with Picts in caves. Waters had more important concerns now.

The next track should perhaps have led the second side of the album. Hearty, melodious and filled with joie de vivre, *Summer '68* was another Rick Wright classic, its melody at once a little haunted but also hummable, its lyrics personal but not too personal, its instrumentation and arrangement verging on brazen, filled with solid brass, rocking drums, and the kind of infectious mid to late 1960s vibe that would never again be part of the Pink Floyd sound. It could easily have sat amongst the songs on *A Saucerful Of Secrets*. Had Love Affair or The Grass Roots got hold of it, it would have been a chart smash. Wright led the verses, but Gilmour came in for the chorus, the opposition of their voices (which could also harmonise beautifully if need be) backed up by the brass section underpinning and Mason's impeccable drumming. The lyrics concerned a random meeting and its consequences, whether because of the group's position on tour with access to all sorts of temptations or via chance, was not certain. Yet the chorus was distinct and direct enough to challenge the listener. How do you feel? It was a good question, one Wright had asked before, and would ask again later in the decade using a more enigmatic phrasing on his delightful solo album.

Gilmour's contribution was *Fat Old Sun*, a languorous number written in his bluesy style, strong on guitars and vibe, with a gorgeous tune and evocative lyrics. Gilmour played all the instruments except keyboards. Opening with images of a late summer afternoon with birds twittering and a heavy heat lying upon the land, it evoked an English idyll as well as any other created by this most English of groups, with its references to distant church bells, twilight and the distinctive odour of new-mown grass. Although these images had been used many times before in art and music, with Gilmour's rolling, strolling musical foundation, they had an extra impact quite outside their content. Gilmour was almost channelling the English pastoral composers with this song, referencing birds, golden sunlight, and English villages at the first signs of the waning of the year. The whole piece was heavy with relaxation, tranquil from beginning to end, set amidst an idealised English landscape which, for most, was a dream, like the song itself. Even when the song picked up a bit of pzazz and reached Gilmour's solo, it was still drowsy, as if uncertain whether or not to wake up or roll over and go back to sleep. And when the group performed it live for the BBC, a night which would be immortalised on the *Floyds Of London* bootleg, Gilmour's voice acquired a knowing melancholy which added to its glorious rumour.

Alan's Psychedelic Breakfast, the concluding track on the LP, was a melange of three pieces intercut with breakfast ruminations from the group's roadie Alan Styles, including what grub he fancied, breakfasts he had enjoyed in the past, and how much he liked marmalade. The kettle was a gas model, not electric, since it could be heard whistling at the end of the first section, *Rise And Shine.* This was keyboard-based music and came mostly from Wright, with the second part, *Sunny Side Up,* performed by Gilmour alone on various guitars. The third part was musically more confident and enjoyable, with a sense of concluding majesty in its descending chord structure. The whole group contributed to this number, though Wright's keyboards assumed prominence in the final arrangement. At the time, this odd track was reluctantly enjoyedby critics, but since then it has come to assume the mantle of one of the group's least popular works. It is really only in the final section that the music coheres into something worth playing more than once; for all the skill and charm of the first two sections, they are hardly necessary accompaniments. Moreover, even the title of this track was unfashionable, generating concern for the position of the band in a post-psychedelic era. By October 1970, when *Atom Heart Mother* was released, even the reaction to psychedelia's loved-up vibe, the darkness and violence of 1968, was a fairly distant memory. That Pink Floyd referenced psychedelia in this piece, and even clung to its central message, was somehow worrying. It spoke of drift – out of touch.

The greatness of the first side, however, and the undoubted charm and melody of a lot of the second side, propelled this LP to the top of the album charts in Britain. It fared less well in America, where the group were still a little-known oddity. But in their home nation, with that cow on the front cover rather than a photo of the group – and even without the group's name – the LP received a good critical response. There was also, albeit only in retrospect and with a pair of binoculars, a first sight of what Pink Floyd might become if they could just give up on the art-whimsy and become a group, rather than a collection of four individuals. Brilliant individuals, yes – but still isolated from the totality of what the group could be. Waters and Gilmour later downplayed the significance of this album, with Waters slagging it off as some half-arsed teenage confection, but those remarks owed more perhaps to what followed than to the actual worth of the music. For, mostly, it *was* great music. Original, striking, enjoyable, filled with melody, insight, and some great playing.

By 1970, the first gleams of progressive rock's gold had come into view, beheld by music fans – especially fans of the serious, worthy LP – with some delight. The Beatles had forwarded the notion of the concept album, King Crimson had shown that stark and astonishing visions could amaze the masses, and Yes were beginning to show what marvels they could create when the band member mix was right. For some groups, it was the notion of a merger between rock and classical music that was the main attraction. This merger would in later years become a symbol of all that was bloated and pretentious about prog, but there was nothing wrong with it in principle, just as there was nothing wrong in principle with the use of sitars or Moog synthesizers. Any instrument could be added to prog's recipes.

For Pink Floyd, floundering somewhat after *Ummagumma*, but with a background in art rock and outré ideas, bringing a full brass section and a choir into their suite for *Atom Heart Mother* felt like a step in the right direction. The choir in particular played an important role, since, although the group's choir used wordless vocalisations, that access to the massed human voice gave the title track of the LP its entry point. Without the brass section, and certainly without the choir, the 20-minute epic would have sounded limp, even uninspired. But the classical music augmentations provided a sense of majesty which propelled the group, though the recording itself was complicated and frustrating, into an arena filled with wonders. This really was new, different and exciting. It was a true melding of rock and non-rock instrumentation, not a cut-and-shut job. Musically, it *worked*. The *Atom Heart Mother Suite* fused two different musical world views into something of delight and excitement. Even today, when listeners worth their salt know the basics of how music is put together in the studio, the position and timbre of the non-music additions, the mixing of the brass section and the choir, the mellifluous quality of Wright's organ playing, and the blues-inflected solos created by Gilmour all merge for them into a marvellous whole.

The suite manifested the opposite of what *Alan's Psychedelic Breakfast* manifested. The former was a complete vision in voice, vibe and timbre: the latter a trio of miscellaneous objects tied together with sonic string. But classical and rock breathed in harmony for the suite.

LP covers during the proto-progressive period began to get artistic. For most of the 1960s, the emphasis had been on photographs of the artist or band, with The Beatles, for instance, depicted on almost every one of their releases. Often, the artistes and their personalities were as much of a draw as their music. The debut Pink Floyd album featured a suitably psychedelic photograph, and the group were again depicted on their next LP in 1968, albeit tiny amidst an ocean of trippy graphics, a cover designed by Storm Thorgerson of Hipgnosis, with whom Pink Floyd would have a notable and long-term relationship. 1969's *Ummagumma* also featured a group portrait, though developed by Hipgnosis into something witty and striking.

But as the 1960s stumbled into 1970, a new mood began to well up in British music. So far, the overwhelming majority of pop and rock influences had come from America, although The Beatles had made a success of selling America's popular music back to it, much improved. But rock 'n' roll and the hippie movement were both authentic American inventions. Progressive rock however, was a home-grown movement, developing from various English roots, not least a dissatisfaction with the whimsy of psychedelia, which anyway fizzled out in the dark year of 1968. But by 1970, a number of new groups had appeared, and their LP covers were different.

Yes had appeared on the music scene after Jon Anderson and Chris Squire got together, powered by hippie mantras, Anderson's intense ambition, and the pair's knack with a tune and their choice of songs to cover. The debut Yes album featured a huge graphic of the band name, while the next featured a surreal work of art. Only their third album in 1970 – rather incongruously, given their subsequent association with painter Roger Dean – featured a group photograph; and a somewhat awkward one at that. Genesis, meanwhile, from their debut proper *Trespass* onwards through their career, used LP covers filled with mysterious paintings and other artwork, while King Crimson, having acquired one of the greatest LP cover paintings of all time for their debut, also used artwork of various kinds which did not include their image. These bands and many others, the vital vanguards of prog rock, showed the way. Their LPs were often concept albums, or, if not, collections of concept songs, for which a mere group photograph on the LP cover was not enough. Their audiences were older, more educated, from a slightly better social class, and there were few, if any, screaming teenagers at their gigs. All this demanded a new approach to the question of album covers.

Pink Floyd felt the same. While the cover to *Ummagumma* was clever, using the Droste Effect in which an image recursively appears within its own borders, from *Atom Heart Mother* onwards, there would be no more cover photographs of the group. The Storm Thorgerson artwork was proving fruitful, even if the subject matter of the early covers, a cow and an ear, was on first inspection a little peculiar. Nevertheless, the notion worked. This progressive stuff was all about the music, not the four group members who made it. Even The Beatles had only experimented once with a non-band cover, for the stark and straightforward *White Album*. Although at the time there was uncertainty about aspects of Pink Floyd's LP cover designs (including from Thorgerson himself), by the time 1973 arrived, there was synergy between cover concept and music concept. That prism and its depiction of refraction are iconic, as is the burning man handshake and the pig flying over Battersea Power Station. No band name, no title, no group photograph were required. The prism was enough. The burning man was enough. The four towers, even without the flying pig, were enough. Those iconic images stood not only for the LPs they graced, they also stood for each of the concepts and all the extraordinary group history surrounding the writing, recording and release of the music. That is a rare thing, but it was particularly clear through the 1970s as the British progressive music movement, exported successfully to America and around the world, acquired greater depth and significance. Only punk burst the bubble, and then not until 1977, by which time the final Waters-era Thorgerson LP cover had been made – for *The Wall* trod new visual territory, and it was not until 1987 that Hipgnosis would return to the fold.

Yet, for all that prog rock was derided by the punks and the post-punks who swiftly followed them, a certain template for LP covers was now fixed in the minds of most working in the music business. LP covers for the debut

Sex Pistols and Stranglers releases were stylised and instantly recognisable, while via The Damned, there came a new mockery of the traditional band photograph. LP sales were increasing, music was becoming a vital part of the British economy, and so the clothes worn by an LP became increasingly important, be that for little-known punks Eater or notorious punks the Sex Pistols. Yet prog rock led the way out of the visual limitations of the 1960s.

Even a collection of songs like those on *Never Mind The Bollocks, Here's The Sex Pistols* was held together by a concept of sorts – the character of the band, the use of found media styles, the status of the Sex Pistols as the most notorious focus of punk. That gut-punch LP cover was designed by Jamie Reid, a man of high principle and unique vision as well as being a vector of social change through art. The ultimate visual icon of punk art is usually considered to be his Queen Elizabeth II image for the single *God Save The Queen*. That image and the prism from *The Dark Side Of The Moon*, though they stand a world apart and could not come from more different backgrounds, are united in that through their visual concepts they epitomise one moment in music history – both of them truly great.

We British are known worldwide for our emotional restraint and the difficulty we have communicating the deeper human verities. We are masters of understatement, repressed even: the infamous "stiff upper lip." How much outstanding art has been made in the service of sending up that British reserve… a vast amount. In television, film, through books and plays, the British way of restraint when it comes to matters of emotion has been a varied and endless source of creative material.

Much of this comes from the rigidity of our social class structure. Men cannot wield power and operate inside such hierarchies without emotional reserve. It is the British way, and especially the English way, because the scope and exploitative potential of such hierarchies, in which tiny numbers of individuals enjoy lives of excess at the expense of the rest of the nation, could not be envisaged without emotional reserve. Emotions are all about conveying human depths, human *value*. They communicate the universal experiences of life. Working in the nineteenth century at the top of the social tree in the midst of the British Empire meant ignoring the abuse of others, ignoring their pain and anguish. *That* is the English way, from which, as Roger Waters had it, came "quiet desperation." We British ignore our emotions because we do not wish to hear what they are telling us: that exploitation is wrong, that colonisation is wrong, that destruction is wrong, that there is no White Man's Burden, and that other cultures, however different from our own, are just as entitled to freedom as we are. If you repress emotion, you can discount the suffering of others.

A quick trawl through four hundred years of British social history shows that the stiff upper lip, stoicism and emotional restraint were non-existent in Shakespeare's time, and only began to gain traction at the beginning of the British Empire. Those two things – global expansion through barbarism and exploitation, and a new emphasis on emotional reserve – are interlinked via a number of social norms which these days we call tradition or conservatism. *That* is also the English way. But it is highly damaging, to those at the receiving end and for those who practice it.

In an interview for Absolute Radio, David Gilmour described the manner of communication used by the four men of Pink Floyd as "slightly dysfunctional," adding that "we don't communicate that well," and that "we're not that good at talking to each other." But he noted that with their instruments they could use "a communication that speaks louder than words."

And they could. Perhaps that English way of struggling with speech and interpersonal relationships gave an extra sparkle of glamour to the music.

Chapter 7

The Broadcast Collection

The Broadcast Collection is a summary of Pink Floyd's early years playing live for various broadcasters, including the BBC. Concerts in France and Germany are also included in this five-disc set, which is minimally packaged but which is far less expensive than the official *Early Years* collection. Released in 2022 by a licensing company based in London, it takes advantage of the fifty-year copyright limit on British recordings, a limit less stringent in Europe. The latest recording here though, comes from halfway through 1970, when the group were still a cult outfit (cult legend as the artwork has it), albeit with new strings to their bows. In 2020, access changed.

As a collection of otherwise unobtainable or expensive recordings offered to fans at a budget price, this is an attractive prospect. Those who buy this kind of material, myself included, know that bootleg recordings and other items are often the ultimate sources of such music, albeit that they are illegally presented. But here the sound quality is good, with much to recommend it – and it is legal. Few fans would complain!

The first of the five CDs covers 1967 and the group hosted by the BBC, variously on *Top Gear*, *Look Of The Week*, and *Tomorrow's World*. These were days of swift and deep social change, musical mayhem too, with psychedelia and the Summer of Love transforming British culture as every sunshine-soaked week passed by. *Top Gear* was an attempt by the BBC to compete with Radio Luxembourg and offshore pirate stations, accessing the cream of the counterculture and introducing the lugubrious tones of John Peel to the nation. Pink Floyd were the perfect vehicle for such presentations.

From *Look Of The Week*, two songs survive, of which the first, *Pow R. Toc H.*, is a thirty-five-second whoop and cry against a rattling guitar chord. The only complete song is *Astronomy Domine*, its opening mechanical voice weirdly comprehensible in this live version. Barrett's falling cry against a descending chord sequence sounds lost in the most thrilling way in comparison with its studio equivalent, and the thrumming guitar work is exciting, with Waters providing some great bass lines. The slide sound is terrific, and maybe Barrett did use a Zippo fag lighter, as legend has it. The backing vocals are more prominent, also giving this version a more frail vibe.

Six songs make up the next set, recorded on 25 September for *Top Gear*. Opener *The Scarecrow* emphasises the percussive elements as Wright's meandering keyboard line drifts this way and that. The tempo is a little slower, but this adds a sense of wonder to the piece, with the vocals and extraordinary lyrics forefront. As the instruments come in, the whole piece acquires that pastoral air for which the group would become known as the 1960s developed. *The Gnome* is more akin to its studio version, with the percussive element retained. The shout of "hooray!" is euphoric and ragged at the same time, countering Barrett's more restrained singing. *Matilda Mother* comes across in this session as a twin of the studio version, the bass fluttering beneath it. As the instrumental part kicks in, Mason's drums come to the fore, and Wright's wah-enhanced keyboard weaves a weird trance across the rock background. It is a terrific performance.

A very early recorded version of *Set The Controls For The Heart Of The Sun* is here introduced by a Radio 1 DJ (not Peel). It is presented more as a strange song than the freakout classic it would later become, though here some of those late 1960s vibes are present. Yet Mason's drums in this version are faster and more rocky, and Waters' vocal is more present and less whispery. *Reaction In G* is another brief excerpt in which the most interesting aspect is the cringeworthy DJ accompaniment; this from a time when DJs were treated like celebrities and felt the need to splatter their chat across the music. "Tell the A.A., my boy!"

Flaming in this session is slow and thoughtful, emphasising the beauty of Barrett's melody. Wright's tinkling keyboard sound is a great match for the lyrics about flying, skies and stars, while the rest of the group provides a solid backing. The guitar part towards the end has a marvellous naivete to it, taking advantage of the chord sequence.

Three months later, and just before Christmas, the group were again *Top Gear* guests, this time singing three songs and offering an updated version of *Pow R. Toc H.,* to the delight of a youthful John Peel. *Vegetable Man* was never released on a Pink Floyd album, though composed and assessed as the year waned. One of Barrett's darkest visions, it tells a tale of breakdown and isolation, causing most critics to consider it, like *Jugband Blues,* to be a document of Barrett's "lost weekend," in which, as legend has it, the LSD straw which broke Barrett's back was experienced. At the very least, it is Barrett describing himself and his condition; just six weeks earlier, he had gone on stage in America to stand still and silent.

Scream Thy Last Scream is simply strange, live yet unlive, somehow whimsical in its psychedelic style, and also eerie, if not outright creepy in lyrics and in tone. It comes across in this BBC version as the fragmented aftermath of a nightmare, with even Wright's half-strangled keyboard solo upping the ante. An extraordinary audio document; and the dynamic instrumental conclusion is amazing. The opening to *Jugband Blues* has a waltztime lilt quite unlike its studio partner, with Barrett's vocal sounding like the musings of a gifted child. As with other versions on this disk, the effect of the melody is enhanced. A trippy, almost unhinged instrumental conclusion adds pathos to the song, which all listeners, knowing the truth of Barrett's condition, would be moved by before the final goodbye, sung with a backing harmony vocal that makes its sadness even more affecting.

Pow R. Toc H. here is powered at first by Wright's wandering piano lines, which rise, soar and fall over the hypnotic band backing. Later, the vocal ululations, shouts and cries have a savage majesty given fuel by the group's collective psychological state. This is a truly psychedelic piece; the listener can hear the drugs in those vocals. Yet towards the end, there is a sense of calm, conveyed by the bass and guitar.

Three days before this *Top Gear* session, the group worked with *Tomorrow's World,* a BBC television programme about advances in technology. For it, they recorded a cover of the standard *Green Onions* and an instrumental, the former slow and rather stoned, the latter featuring a whirring Hammond part, thunking drums, and a wah-wah guitar solo of great, albeit sparse, beauty.

Disk two kicks off with four tracks introduced by John Peel from a 1968 session recorded on 25 June at Piccadilly Studios. The opener is an early version of *Careful With That Axe, Eugene* (aka *Murderotic Woman*), beginning with plenty of cymbal work and Wright's usual meandering organ solo. Gilmour's guitar darts this way and that, but there is a confidence to it – and a lack of Barrettness – which stands out, especially when it cuts loose. This track is short, however. The feeling of unhappiness is what Peel associates with *The Massed Gadgets Of Hercules*, which, in essence, is a compressed version of *A Saucerful Of Secrets*, recently released at the time. This seven-minute version does show that the group still had something special, for all that their main songwriter had departed. Mason's drums kick in alongside a rolling, thunking piano, before more guitar comes in, this time mimicking Barrett to the max. The intensity of this music, perhaps here more formal than on the LP, is obvious, not least when the drum part closes and the weird anthem at the end hoves into view, announced by a whirring organ. That classic chord sequence never lets the listener down…There is no chorus on this live version, though some distant voices are heard, but the massed ranks of keyboards do ramp up the emotional content; and it is no accident that Peel at the end comments on this music "coming out of churches." Clearly, he was moved. *Let There Be More Light* in this session version opens with a bouncy feel, a lightness which evaporates the moment Gilmour's voice sings. It is a classic Floyd merging of mystical and psychedelic, so redolent of the LP, with Gilmour's guitar paving the way for what was to come over the next couple of years. The last session track is Wright's gorgeous song *Julia Dream*, here played with an open-eyed innocence, even when the lyrics get strange. Wright pulls exactly the right timbre out of his keyboard: soft and enigmatic.

On 3 November, the group recorded a single track for the BBC programme *Omnibus, Set The Controls For The Heart Of The Sun*. This version makes the most of the riff and pounding drums, but Waters' vocal wanders in and out of key. It is not their finest version. The drums and keyboard solo however, do in due course lift the track, as Gilmour finds something (it is hard to say what) to fit, eventually settling on his wah-wah pedal.

Earlier in 1968, the group had performed in Bouton Rouge, France, where they played a storming set of four songs. Opening with *Astronomy Domine*, drums clatter and bass thrums, but it is strange to hear a new voice singing, and an unfamiliar guitar. The vocals are mixed low, though the descending wails sound great. Yet the energy of the group is palpable, especially in the instrumental section. *Flaming* comes across as a naive yet intense children's song, its rock beat sitting just underneath. Here converted into a harder sound, the song's new vibe does work: a bit unhinged, a bit rock'n'roll, a bit odd. This is a uniquely propulsive version. *Set The Controls For The Heart Of The Sun* is here more floaty than in other versions, the drums and guitar merging to perfection as they underpin Waters' vocal, here assured, and even a little spooky as he drawls and drags his vowels. Then Wright enters the mix with a semi-Eastern organ solo, rippling over the band; one of his best. *Let There Be More Light* in this performance is up-tempo and brash, with Mason on fine form.

Three months later, the group were in Italy, recording two of their earliest tracks, *Astronomy Domine* and *Interstellar Overdrive*, for *Rome Goes Pop*. The first is sped up slightly, with Gilmour-esque guitar and huge amounts of chutzpah. *Interstellar Overdrive* is given a rock thrashing, full of the weirdest sonic inserts, voice and guitar, which fade as Mason and Waters enter the fray. An oddly restrained jam ensues, full of stops and starts, with excellent interplay between Wright and Gilmour. It is a bit like listening to a mash-up of early Floyd and early Tangerine Dream. As Gilmour's twisted guitar ducks and dives, Waters brings in the second main riff and the group heads off into space. This version emphasises the sonic weirdness of the track, sacrificing a bit of coherence along the way, though this is without doubt a compelling version.

At the end of the year, the group again found themselves encamped at the BBC, this time in Maida Vale, there to record four tracks. *Point Me At The Sky* showcased Gilmour's vocals to excellent effect, while the rest of the group were on sparkling form, with Wright proffering a suitably cosmic organ section. It was an assured demonstration of how tight the group could be live. *Embryo* is here given an exotic sheen, rooted in strummed guitar and another of Wright's whirring, ethereal keyboard parts; it also emphasises what a beautiful melody the song has. Coming across as half pastoral, half psychedelic, the song epitomises classic 1960s Pink Floyd: gorgeous, strange, mysterious. *Baby Blue Shuffle In D Major* is an acoustic oddity based on fingerpicked guitar and drifting keyboards. A version of *Interstellar Overdrive* concludes the set, this one more rhythmically formal than others, albeit with a rare lightness of touch. Waters and Wright work well together, with all sorts of avian guitar sounds leaping around the mix. A dramatic rock insert interrupts the mood, leading to a hectic section reminiscent in places of ELP.

It is, however, another demonstration that this group were at the forefront of psychedelic improvisation, with the concluding Wright/Mason interplay of a high order, and the change from the middle part to the return of the descending chord sequence masterfully handled by all four.

This disk is fascinating because it documents the transition from Barrett's guitar to Gilmour's guitar. In places, Gilmour mimicked the classic Barrett sounds, but elsewhere he was his own musician, and a fine one at that. Often the group betrayed nothing of the uncertainty they were facing, and many of their recorded sessions and performances were still of the highest standard.

By 1969, Pink Floyd were becoming a honed and often mesmerising live act. The legacy of Syd Barrett was in the past, David Gilmour was a fixture, and there were new horizons to explore. 1969 would be the year of much live work. The third and fourth disks of *The Broadcast Collection* showcase this trippy, proto-progressive direction, opening with two exceptional recordings from a January gig in Paris. *Set The Controls For The Heart Of The Sun* that night was as finely wrought as any of their performances, with virtuoso keyboard work from Wright, and Waters making the most of his spectral vocals. Sea bird sounds added to the mystery, while Mason's hypnotic tom-tom work held the edifice together. *A Saucerful Of Secrets* meanwhile, was on that night the epitome of spaced-out cosmic intensity, sounding, in fact, remarkably similar to the studio version; almost identical in places.

Four months later, the group performed a full set at Southampton University's Old Rectory, opening with a blast from the past: *Astronomy Domine.* This version is tight and it rocks out, with the vocals and harmony vocals matching to perfection, even with the addition of a few screeches. Yet in the heavy guitar work, this was very much a post-Barrett version, even given the chilled keyboard section. *Careful With That Axe, Eugene* ("It has a very quiet start." – Waters) is in this performance more supple than others, with the keyboard and guitar interplay superb, all supported by Mason's rimshot percussion. As part-improvised music, this had few peers at the time, as the group grasped for a new direction and novel sounds. The build-up is handled with sudden intensity, Gilmour's voice echoing his immense guitar solo, a trick he would employ for some time, both live and in the studio. Another return to past glories comes in the form of *Interstellar Overdrive,* here given a cosmic veneer, opening with spacey keyboards before the descending riff kicks in. Again, this is a rock version of the music, hardly psychedelic, with plenty of wailing guitars and Mason battering his drumkit; in places it even sounds un-Floyd, in particular during a staccato guitar solo section. The group were pushing this cut to the edge of its sonic territory. *Green Is The Colour* meanwhile moves into those sun-dappled and bucolic fields that the group made their own for a couple of years. Gilmour, singing, invests the song with just the right amount of purity, almost sweetness. It is a terrific performance, complemented by Wright's shimmering keyboards. *Beset By Creatures Of The Deep,* into which the song segues, begins as a slow tempo instrumental with Gilmour's slide guitar to the fore; another inspired solo, hinting at those marvellous guitar parts he would devise in 1971. Soon, however, it morphs into an up-tempo rocker, which then fades into spacey nothingness. The version of *A Saucerful Of Secrets* is quite different from the LP version, here opening with exotic slide guitar and keyboard sounds, and clearly improvised, before a darker, denser vibe emerges, carried by Mason and Gilmour. The sound here is absolutely freaked out – intense, mind-battering music of great power. As Mason's snare patterns change, the music swoops and dives, like some immense mechanical roc, harassing travellers. There is a hint in the paranoia of this version of *On The Run,* which, though that track sounds so different, evokes the same feeling in the listener. An exceptional performance, this one, merging mixing desk tricks into the sound, too. And the cosmic section at the end, announced by a Rick Wright keyboard part of great beauty, allows the listener to drift off into ethereal, enigmatic space, listening to Gilmour's wordless, fearless vocals…

These performances illustrate quite what a difference David Gilmour made to the band as he devised and sophisticated his position in the group. Not only was his guitar style so different from Barrett's, but his voice and manner were too. This was a sea-change, not the replacement of one man with another. A new Pink Floyd was being forged.

The fourth disk begins on 12 May, when Pink Floyd played at the Paris Theatre in London, opening with one of their pastoral classics, *Daybreak,* aka *Grantchester Meadows.* This soft, subtle take on one of their most melodic songs benefits from light backing vocals and taped birdsong sounding like that used for the equally gorgeous *Cirrus Minor.* Waters provides one of his best live vocals, filled with a knowing wisdom, emphasised by images such as kingfishers diving into streams. When Wright's piano comes in, the mood is perfect. *Nightmare*, better known as *Cymbeline*, is sung by Gilmour, the mood still summer-soft and bucolic. Wright's keyboard solo is marvellous in its melancholic spaciness, with Mason and Wright providing undercurrents of ghostly mystery – a superb performance of one of their best early songs. *The Narrow Way III* fades in with Gilmour providing a vocal of great clarity, both in his natural voice and through falsetto. The ominous melody and chord sequence of the verse oppose the more melodic chorus to perfection. These songs showcase music that does not have those quirky Barrett melodies, yet their melodic strength cannot be doubted. *Green Is The Colour,* meanwhile, here performed with almost wilful melancholy, continues the mood of reflective ambiguity, even when Gilmour sends out a solo emphasised by Wright's drifting, shimmering keyboards. For fans of the pastoral Pink Floyd, these four live versions are a treat and a delight.

On 20 July 1969, Neil Armstrong and Buzz Aldrin became the first men on the Moon. Accompanying the BBC coverage, fronted by James Burke, the group were asked to perform live music, here presented as *Moonhead*. The sound quality suggests a front-of-television recording, but it is no less fascinating for that. The opening sections are spacey and light, but there is a hint of a bass line which in four years time would become world famous. As presenter voices fade, the tempo of the improvisation increases, and the source of that bass line and E/A/B chord sequence becomes clear. It is the middle section of *Money*. In due course, a wailing voice enters the mix. As the track lightens and drifts, Wright's oscillating keyboards, drenched in reverb and echo, carry the listener into lunar orbit, with Gilmour's slide guitar flying alongside. Meanwhile, Waters and Mason keep up the thrumming, almost mechanical backing; a great contrast of two opposites. This piece is only seven minutes long, but it is a compelling listen.

Later that year, the group played at the Essener Pop & Blues Festival in Germany. Opening with *Careful With That Axe, Eugene,* this version emphasises Waters' floating, keening, sometimes wailing vocal, while Wright's keyboards have a Terry Riley-like intensity. This is a heavy version! The guitar solo has a strangulated quality about it, un-Gilmour almost, and a strange staccato feel. In this version, the contrast between the soft and loud parts is extreme. The second track is *A Saucerful Of Secrets,* again playing on the potential for contrast between cosmic and dramatic, with the spacey sections floating free, the psychedelic section piercing and cymbal-drenched, and the tom-tom powered middle section filled with noise like dying space vehicles and other futuristic disasters; it sounds like an interplanetary collision, Gilmour's guitar again taking a piercing timbre. There is an almost brutal intensity to this evocation of dense, cosmic chaos. The third section brings Gilmour's voice up again, with Mason providing a funereal drum accompaniment that soon turns into a full rock assault; very effective, especially with Waters' backing. A terrific version all the way to the 100% rock conclusion.

In the final disk (1970), it is very much the post-1960s Pink Floyd playing, with not a hint of psychedelic whimsy. The dual Gilmour/Wright vocals are a template for the next decade, with Gilmour's guitar fully into blues mode. Opening with *Embryo,* this is a great BBC sound, everything clear and well balanced, the group showing confidence and authority in their playing, which is simultaneously as tight and as loose as any Floyd fan could wish for. The taped recordings of an infant work well above Wright's softly looping organ solo, and Waters making the most of his bass part. The famous *Echoes* guitar sound (an accident of effects unit plugging) makes an early appearance, and there is lots going on elsewhere. What strikes the listener is the confidence the group have in their live music; leaps forward in all respects. John Peel was right – fans must have been looking forward to the concert for weeks.

Gilmour is to the fore with *Fat Old Sun,* introduced by Peel with reference to the optimistic vibe of the music. The steady beat underpins a vocal with just the right amount of wide-eyed wonder. Mason here takes his drumming up and down a few notches in time with the dynamics of the song; also perfectly judged, while the guitar solo is classic bend-and-blues Gilmour ("Really beautiful." – John Peel). The group's version of *Green Is The Colour* also has a bluesy feel, as Gilmour bends his vocal intonation through this supremely summery song. The backing is as light as a feather, but it is Gilmour who is the focus and star of this gorgeous performance.

Careful With That Axe, Eugene opens with the softest of keyboard sounds, as Mason's cymbals begin to tap out the ominous rhythm and guitar notes float this way and that. That wailing voice and spectral whisper are hypnotic in their form, with the darker, crazier elements on the very edge of hearing.

Yet when the central section breaks out, craziness is let loose, an extra layer of mixer delay extending the vocal sound into Hell itself. The task of returning the music to Earth is given to Wright… and then the diminished conclusion fades into silence, before lengthy and appreciative applause.

If follows, Waters playing acoustic guitar while Wright supports on bass and organ simultaneously, Peel commenting "that should be worth watching" in his most wry tones. Waters' vocal is frail and regretful, offering up the essence of his song.

Concluding this set, the group present the *Atom Heart Mother* suite. The brass parts are subtly different from the LP recording, indicating a live element. Tapes provide the horse and explosion sounds. The second theme is also played live, by a brass soloist, replacing the cellist, and there is a lovely handover when Gilmour's slide solo comes in. The choir used on the LP is also recreated live here, at first with female voices, with later male voices making a marvellous lower register harmony. When the band returns, it all coheres, Mason's drums sounding particularly good. The subsequent guitar solo is shorn of its studio effects, but still sounds awesome, and the choir make an excellent go of the "crazy vocal section" towards the end. More recorded tapes enhance the penultimate section, while the final part is suitably triumphant in tone. As a live performance of a complex piece, this could hardly be bettered, and it is a rewarding listen.

The Broadcast Collection not only offers cash-strapped fans a five disk set at one twentieth of the price of the official collection, it serves to document three important aspects of this part of the group's career. The first is that transition away from Syd Barrett's inimitable melodies, all of them unique to him and seeming to come from some quixotic corner of his personal galaxy. This is not to say that the melodic core of the group's songs diminished after his loss; it did not. But a move from psychedelic whimsy to darker, denser rock theatrics is obvious as this collection of radio sessions and live recordings passes by. The joy of the Summer of Love was soon replaced by something less playful. Pink Floyd managed to transform that playfulness into a bucolic charm, epitomised by songs like *Cirrus Minor* and *Grantchester Meadows*, but there were bleaker visions too, not least the emotionally compelling *Careful With That Axe, Eugene*. The second change began with the arrival of David Gilmour, whose natural guitar style soon took the group away from

Barrett's high-psychedelic wizardry into a more bluesy zone. With him taking many of the lead vocals too, the stage was set for the appearance of a remodelled Floyd.

The third aspect of these years is the influence the group had on other bands. One in particular serves to demonstrate this: Tangerine Dream. In the late 1960s, their groundbreaking electronic albums *Phaedra* and *Rubycon* were still a good few years in the future. Tangerine Dream, with the Floyd-loving Edgar Froese at the helm, were an improvising psych-rock band with an ever-shifting membership, albeit with Froese never vacating the director's seat. One year before Pink Floyd's appearance at the Essener Pop & Blues Festival, an early incarnation of Tangerine Dream played there, their music inspired by the improvising skill of the English group, and their part psychedelic, part progressive music. Some of the Ohr Records LPs that Tangerine Dream released in the early 1970s could almost feature alternate Pink Floyd cuts, especially on *Alpha Centauri* and *Atem*. Pink Floyd, though a cult group making art music, were highly influential at home and in Europe.

Chapter 8

Meddle

Touring commitments meant that the group struggled to find the format and vibe for a new album. But there was another obstacle. Although the departure of Syd Barrett had occurred a few years before, there was still no central focus, either within the band or connecting their disparate earlier albums. Individually, those post-Barrett albums – especially *Atom Heart Mother* and *A Saucerful Of Secrets* – were marvellous LPs, but they spoke of a band having a bit of a wander through half-recognised and poorly understood territory: a musically signposted Sunday afternoon stroll. They were experimenting, and that was fine. But although the group members had worked with one another for some time, they were, in classic English mode, friendly strangers to one another. Reserve and understatement was their style. Their experimentation therefore, was somewhat hit-and-miss. The group was a unit, and a much-appreciated one across the nation, but something about them was still rather unfocused. In years to come, that focus would be provided by Roger Waters' lyrical themes and concepts, but in 1971, that structure was still some way off.

The group, however, were becoming a tight and enthralling live act, and the time had come for some of that brilliance to find its way into the recording studio. Having negotiated a new contract that offered them a reduced royalty rate but offered them unlimited time in the studio, the option of using their recording studio in a similar manner to The Beatles arrived. This, in essence, was the link between the wandering, unfocused Floyd – terrific cult band – and the creative unit that became a behemoth of the 1970s – prog rock masters. All four members of the group worked in a place somewhere between music and art, with music as their vehicle, but their instincts were to expand creative horizons into artistic directions which could feed into music. Often, Mason would be the instigator of such sessions. One set of experiments had them using non-musical instruments to create pieces, but this was ditched pretty soon. They jammed on tour and they had the eight-track EMI studio to play in, yet all those facilities, all that experience and their own quirky musicality – still set in psychedelic mode, with the Summer of Love only three years behind them – brought them five short songs which could hardly be more different. The omens were not exactly promising.

Atom Heart Mother consisted of a side-long epic, a trio of songs, and a psychedelic assortment with a breakfast theme. These were disparate pieces, but somehow all found a place on the album, which cohered well in the listener's mind once it was assimilated. The five songs worked up for side one of *Meddle* were not only disparate, they managed to oppose one another; no overarching theme, no structure, no overall vision. Individually, a couple of them were good, even great, but side by side and numbered one to five, they stood like a tricky double-S bend on a narrow Alpine road. For the listener, navigation would not be easy.

One Of These Days came across as a dark, even brutal piece of thunking, stroppy psychedelia, founded on Waters' bass line put through a tape delay unit. Its chord sequence was dramatic, but somewhat uninspired. The track had the feel of a storm and its aftermath; but no wholesome storm. This one featured greasy rain, damaging, gusty winds, discordant thunder and random flashes of backwards lightning. Listening to it was an experience of gothic intensity, good for a few listens but not exactly a grower. Yet it was the right opener for the album, its unusual sound, propulsive rhythm and fine playing recommending it. Nick Mason provided the voice at the end. There was no digital equipment in 1971, but the use of ferric tape meant that speed changes could be utilised to change the quality of voices or instruments. The Beatles at Abbey Road were the originators of such effects in rock music. Pink Floyd, working in the same stable, also used them. Mason's voice was recorded at twice the usual speed, and he used a falsetto tone. When this was replayed at normal speed, the unique, growling effect was achieved. That single, threatening line, the only vocal on the track, summarised the sombre, brooding quality of the piece. It spoke of damage under duress, of violence and dark, dark thoughts.

Pillow Of Winds was diametrically opposed. As near to a straight love song as this band ever came, its soft folk vibe, beautiful playing and memorable tune made it gorgeous. Moreover, it had that soft, golden afternoon haze that some music recorded at the start of the 1970s had. Its sound was akin to the end of the apple harvest during a warm weekend; mild weather unexpected after frosts of autumn; sunshine and haze, sleep and love, and soft eiderdown. Reminiscent of some of Rick Wright's songs, it was, in fact, written by Gilmour and Waters.

Individually striking though these songs were, they sat uncomfortably alongside each other, like a grumpy, balding old parent and their gorgeous, golden-haired hippy daughter. But another sidestep into dissonance arrived with the third track, *Fearless*. This was a slow-paced number laced with allusions to football through the song *You'll Never Walk Alone,* which took over the piece at its conclusion. The chord sequence and the sound of the chiming guitars were wonderful, but the lyrics were obscure and the overall feel unassuming. Certainly, a feeling of soft languor carried on from the previous track, an impression of its sonic warmth, but the football sounds and the length of the track – six very long minutes – meant that such impressions were trampled over. It was not a bad song; just not a good one. John Peel surely adored it, though.

The two tracks which followed could be called throwaway. It was downhill from *A Pillow Of Winds,* all the way to the awkward, disappointing bottom. The group had spent time in the south of France, which made for some marvellous photographs used in expensive, hardcover books later on, but which also resulted in Waters' faux-jazz *San Tropez,* with its shuffle beat and forgettable lyrics. In fact, it might be better to call this set words, not lyrics. The song was filler; there could be no doubt of that. On the album, it felt dissonant in vibe, tone, context and goal. It sounded like Roger Waters auditioning for duties in some hastily assembled hotel dining room combo, a Pink Floyd so vacuous the manager retitled them Blanched Floyd. *Seamus,* meanwhile, would have embarrassed a school music project done by Year 9 pupils on their first assignment. Noting that Steve Marriott's dog would join in with some kinds of music, the group recorded a blues number in which the hound did exactly that. Film exists of them playing this number, with Rick Wright holding the dog microphone and looking uncomfortable. Gilmour plays his harmonica semi-oblivious. Even the arch-provocateur

Waters looks perplexed – which is saying something. A top contender for Pink Floyd's worst piece.

Yet for every black there is a white, for every disaster a triumph. That's just the way of things. The rule holds in music as everywhere else, a point illustrated par excellence by *Meddle*. Side one was listenable; partly. Side two was a revelation.

Echoes came together in pieces, with some music being discarded, but when it was complete at over twenty-three minutes, it stood – and to some fans still stands – as the perfect, most adored, most revered Pink Floyd song. Moving from one of the most recognisable openings in all rock music, through one of its most beautiful melodies, to one of its best rock-out middle sections, via a transcendent reprise and conclusion, its deep lyrical themes were matched by its wonderful music, creating something quite breathtaking.

During 1971, the group became dissatisfied with their eight-track recording facilities, as their creative urges outstripped the machines they were using. Elsewhere in London, sixteen-track recording machines were available. The group took all the best parts and pieces from their eight-track reels and transferred them to the new locale. For this reason, a new possibility opened up. Some of the suite *Atom Heart Mother* had to be recorded all in one go, which led to understandable problems of band members being unsure where in the piece they were during its recording. *Echoes* was the first long track that the group could record in parts, overdubbing and extending in a way which would become standard in the near future, not least for the masterpiece which followed *Meddle*.

The piece began with Rick Wright sitting at a concert grand piano with the microphone output fed into a Leslie cabinet (a set-up utilised by George Martin and his team when John Lennon requested that the sound of his voice be mutated into that of a mountain-top Tibetan lama for *Tomorrow Never Knows*). When he played, a single note hung and reverberated, evoking submarine depths, lonely and enigmatic. This opening is built into the introduction to the song, then to the twin-vocal melody, sung by Gilmour and Wright. Gilmour, later, following Wright's tragic death, called him his soul-brother; the union of their voices can be called exalted on this rendition. It is exquisite; perhaps their finest joint recording. Gilmour also happened to be one of the best double-tracking vocalists of his generation, with an uncanny ability to match a first take with a perfect second. The piece then mutated into a funk-filled instrumental, which decayed into enigmatic ambience before returning for the song reprise. All in all, the singing on *Echoes* stirred the listener's emotions as perhaps no Floyd song had until then. This was hairs-up-on-the-arms stuff. It was sublime.

When on 30 September 1971 the BBC recorded the group at the Paris Theatre in London in front of an enthusiastic audience, the final song was *Echoes*. John Peel, discarding his usual lugubrious tones, explained that the group's roadies, Pete and Scott, had described the piece as "an extraordinarily good number." They were not wrong there.

The lyrical concerns of *Echoes* were also rather different from previous work. In the piece, Waters wished to address ideas of contact, communication and empathy. Opening with beautifully evoked images of sea and shoreline, the scene is set for one of his classic lines, referring to strangers passing in the street, but the irony was that the group itself could be like this. All at this stage, however, happens by chance – two human gazes crossing each other at random. Empathy is invoked when the two participants realise they are equals of each other. This is a foundation of consciousness, the human outcome of empathy, which in the song is described as two people hand-in-hand attempting the great human task of understanding. At the end, the song returns to images of sunlight and skies, cloudless upon waking, and windows and bright morning light. The final image of the song is of windows flung open in a joyous act of communication.

This seamless whole, a merging of inspirational lyrics, beautiful music, fabulous playing and some of the most memorable sound choices in progressive rock, combined to form something magical. Pink Floyd had recorded marvellous songs before, trailblazing and unique, but never before had they crossed the boundary into magic. Yet *Echoes* was the real thing: a revelatory triumph forged by a band suddenly casting aside their arty pretensions for something with emotional depth. Great depth, in fact, as conveyed by words and music in perfect harmony. But even the sound choices were inspired. The submarine ping was instantly recognisable. The guitar solos were as fluid as any Gilmour had so far committed to tape. The cawing crows and reverberated effects in the middle section were as thrilling and mysterious as any so far used by the group. But perhaps the most spine-tingling choice was the choir rising up into the wide, blue, inaccessible empyrean, a sound that ended the piece alongside a last, lonely ping.

That choir sound, recorded using a pair of tape machines, utilises an audio illusion known as a Shepard Tone. This occurs when a sound is superposed upon itself in octaves. When the lowest note of the set is raised or lowered in pitch, the illusion known as the Shepard Scale is created, of the entire sound rising or falling, yet apparently with no end point – which would be expected at around 20kHz. The choir on *Echoes* did precisely that. The effect was achieved by placing the two machines in opposite corners of the studio, setting one machine to play and the other to record. This introduced a time delay between the two, much like that created by the two tape heads of the Echorec unit used by the group. The spine-tingling quality of this sound was the perfect elegiac timbre for the conclusion of the piece.

The other extraordinary sound was that created for the middle section. This was an impressionistic, ambient interlude filled with Tangerine Dream-like floating bass frequencies, as used by Edgar Froese on the group's early Ohr Records albums. Cawing crows introduced a haunting quality to this part. Following an accidental reversal of leads into Gilmour's wah-wah pedal, where the guitar was connected to the pedal output and the amplifier to its input, sounds not unlike seagulls shrieking could be created, which, when placed into different reverbs and with reduced volume, gave the effect of a flock of alien birds hovering in macabre flight above and around the listener. This effect had been utilised on the non-album live cut *Embryo*, but on *Echoes* it achieved maximum impact.

For David Gilmour, *Echoes* was the song in which his guitar playing acquired maximum Gilmourness, after which his sound became instantly recognisable to the masses. The opening solo after the first rendition of the song could not have been played by anyone else. But what made a Gilmour guitar solo so characteristic?

There are several guitarists through the 1960s and 1970s to whom this question could be applied. Jimmy Page was one, Steve Hillage, Steve Howe, and Mike Oldfield, too. When everything is considered, it usually comes down to matters of vibrato and note bending. Jimmy Page bent his notes in a particular way, with a comparatively slow vibrato. Even if he was not playing his signature Gibson guitar, that individual way of emphasising emotional content was his alone. Steve Hillage also had his own way of creating vibrato, especially on high notes, and particularly after he had bent it upwards, instantly characterised by its wide pitch range; a style recognisable regardless of which band he was playing in. A Hillage solo could be played shorn of music and easily be recognised. Likewise, a Steve Howe solo, with its glissando effects especially, could immediately be recognised by the listener. As for Mike Oldfield, his intense style of vibrato, moving his hand horizontally, made his solo parts unique. All these guitarists and others arrived at their particular sound to express through their instrument what lay inside them: emotions, feelings. In these two decades, there were fewer groups and fewer musicians. Now the internet is flooded with anonymous guitarists, all of whom sound similar. This is a consequence of the internet itself, but it also speaks of how rock music in its early days was a field in which true individuality could be manifested and broadcast. In part, this was because the field was small; yet what youthful guitarist today has a soloing style as instantly recognisable as Mike Oldfield's?

For Gilmour, the key to expression through his electric guitar was bending notes. A Gilmour solo, including that stunning example after the first rendition of the song in *Echoes,* is one in which almost every note is bent into another one, or, if not, is a note emerging from the bending of the previous. Gilmour's solos, therefore, as the band explored its artistic landscape, acquired a fluidity which marked them out. That continual fluid motion from bending notes applied throughout solos, not just for a few high drama notes at the upper end of the fretboard. Moreover, Gilmour sometimes left a note hanging a tiny bit off the destination note, almost like a quarter tone in Middle Eastern music, which to the Western ear granted it a unique, exotic character. Exploring those unusual pitches at the outer edges of just intonation augmented Gilmour's already unique sound, which in that mellifluous solo for *Echoes* gave it a plangent quality quite unlike any other guitarist's. Gilmour really could do melancholy, regret and elegy.

A guitar solo is not just an expression of technique or the instrument itself. Those early progressive rock guitar heroes were, in most cases, trying to connect the feel of the song with their own inner world. Creativity is a human act unknown amongst animals, though, of course, animals can arrive at creative solutions to problems. But music is a human art. It derives from our status as conscious individuals. When David Gilmour created, then played the guitar solo for *Echoes* he was linking the warm, empathic, but also quite rueful tone of the lyrics, with their emphasis on people failing to connect and empathise with one another, with his own inner state. Such creative musicality is a function of sensitivity to mood and vibe. Gilmour sensed the feel of the song, and not just through its lyrics – the melody has a distinct pensive quality about it, very much in a minor mood. Through his guitar playing and his ability to represent emotional feeling through his style, he echoed the tone of the piece. He linked his own feelings, deeply felt, with those of the song. It was the perfect match. And when the chords moved into major mode and he brought a second guitar in, there was a new sense of warmth and positivity, yet never too far from that sense of regret. It was one of his most moving guitar solos.

One year had passed following the release of *Atom Heart Mother*. Indeed, since signing to EMI, the group had released one LP per year, plus the curio of the *More* film soundtrack in 1969. But *Meddle* seemed afterwards to contain a signpost to a brand new landscape. Its cover, however, was designed by the group's regular art collective, Hipgnosis. In blue and orange, it featured a close-up of a human ear, overlaid with images of ripples in water. These ripples represented waves of human communication through sound – the empathy explored by Waters in his incisive lyrics for *Echoes*. There was continuity, but forward motion also.

In 1971, Pink Floyd were not quite the arty cult group of the late 1960s nor quite the half psychedelic, half progressive sonic explorers of 1970. Although only one year had passed since *Atom Heart Mother*, some new form of group action had raised them from their earlier status as noble experimenters in rock music. They achieved this with no input from their record label, representatives of which would occasionally pop by with a bottle of wine. Of course, the music had always been noteworthy, and it had sold sufficiently well for the group to be retained. But *Meddle* was the product of a new mental horizon. Its first side was akin to a table on which five ingredients lay. Its second side was that same table set with a banquet created by a master chef. *Meddle* paved the way from musicians with creative wit and musical integrity to an exceptional group, for whom everything after *Echoes* would be qualitatively different.

Chapter 9

Obscured By Clouds

At the beginning of 1972, when the group was preparing for the iconic album to come, another film soundtrack offer came their way from Barbet Schroeder, with whom they had worked a few years earlier on his film *More*. This one was similar in vibe, two people undertaking a spiritual adventure in Papua New Guinea, and it was called *La Vallée*.

The quartet accepted the offer. For *More,* they had viewed a rough cut of the film and taken approximate timings from it in order to write and prepare the music. Now, at the start of the year, they were touring in the Far East and beginning to sound out ideas for *The Dark Side Of The Moon,* but it was decided there was time available to finish enough music for the soundtrack, so the project went ahead. Two recording sessions and a fortnight were enough. There were songs, instrumental pieces, and a few miscellaneous items, one of which would be released in America as a single.

Obscured By Clouds, the LP created for release in summer that year, had ten tracks set out over forty minutes. The opener was a Floyd classic written by Waters and Gilmour, using ominous drone sounds created by Wright using the EMS synthesizer that he had acquired from the BBC. The vibe was one of peril, underpinned by those drones and Mason's drum pattern. Twinned guitars, one playing a harmony part, came in to establish a theme. The tempo was slow and somewhat threatening – a great beginning. *When You're In* was a riff-based group composition with an improvised feel; nothing much was going on, but it was sufficient for supporting film music.

Burning Bridges, by contrast, was by far the best song on the album, and could even have found a place on the next LP. A gorgeous melody penned by Wright and Waters was sung by Gilmour and Waters, separately and in harmony, while a key change elevated this melody into something special. There was a hint here of some of those soft, pastoral songs placed on side 1 of *Meddle,* particularly *Pillow Of Winds.* A dreamy guitar solo rounded off the track, elevating it higher still. This is without doubt one of the group's finest songs of the period, displaying their mastery of songwriting and illustrating how their grasp of the bucolic style, which by now they had used for a few years, made such tracks so successful. Schroeder was lucky to acquire it.

The Gold It's In The... was an up-tempo rocker with a Gilmour vocal, written by him and Waters, a song that came across as an American-styled piece, even to the extent of sounding quite un-Floyd. This could be imagined as a song that escaped the clutches of Tom Petty. With riffing guitars and Waters providing one of his best bass parts, the song rocked out in spectacular style, not least the guitar solo provided by Gilmour. *Wot's... Uh The Deal*, also written by the pair, provided the chill after the wig-out, another light and dreamy song with a Gilmour vocal. Gilmour's slide guitar was well in evidence here, and Wright provided a fine piano outro for the track.

Mudmen was an instrumental version of *Burning Bridges.* Prepared by Wright with Gilmour's aid, it followed the chord sequence and melody of the song but emphasised the keyboards and the EMS synthesiser much more. Complex, affecting and beautiful, it was another superb example of how such music could come together quickly when the inspiration was there. A classic, piercing Gilmour solo in the style that he would later become renowned for was laid over the top of this instrumental piece, contributing to its artistic success.

Childhood's End was a Gilmour solo work, its brief introduction based on a drum pattern and lots of synthesisers, instruments the group were becoming accustomed to despite the relative earliness of synth development. The full group came in later, Gilmour singing another fine melody. He also recorded another superb guitar solo, one that made use of the "Gilmour bend" string technique, which, as the decade passed, would become one of the most obvious signatures of his style.

Free Four was a Waters song; quirky, leftfield, lyrically obtuse. Yet, for all that, something of what was to come the following year may have been on his mind. The lyrics were all about life and death, getting eighty years if you're lucky, being in a band at the top of the tree touring America... yet was that lifestyle all a trap? With its rockstar guitar solo, eccentric – but eminently hummable – tune, and ironic insouciance, the song was classic Waters. That this nugget of irony was released in America as a single only served to emphasise the ironic nature of the song. It failed to trouble the charts there.

Stay was a Waters and Wright composition, sung by Waters with another fine piece of slide guitar by Gilmour, this time accentuated by a wah-wah pedal. Slow and downbeat, the lyrics alluded to an unnamed girl. The LP concluded with *Absolutely Curtains,* a full group composition, whose soft, spacey opening immediately made the listener cast their thoughts back to Wright's 1960s keyboard set-up. The beautiful, chilled vibe recalled these masters of space music at their finest, revving up halfway through before blissing out again. In the only external sound to feature in this music, a recording of Papua New Guinea chanting concluded the track.

That Pink Floyd were asked to compose film music – albeit by a director they knew and had worked with before – illustrated how, in 1972, they stood on a tightrope between their old cult status and something altogether different. After 1973 and the subsequent colossal success, there were no more group forays into French recording studios for a fortnight's enjoyable improvisation and recording, though Wright and Gilmour would later record solo albums across the English Channel. With Waters taking over as lyricist and wielder of concepts, Pink Floyd became what they are recognised as today. Few directors would have had the nerve to ask them for film soundtrack music. The group's output would diminish from one album per year to one every two. The focus changed, the reception changed, the perception of the group by their fans changed. A new, elevated status was in the making.

The cult group known only a handful of years earlier as The Pink Floyd Sound were about to bestride the world.

Chapter 10

The Dark Side Of The Moon

Echoes was the game-changer. Between the departure of Syd Barrett and the recording of that epic twenty-three-minute piece, the group had floundered a little, trying different directions, aligning themselves with the space race, and slowly becoming bound up with the burgeoning progressive rock movement. They were artists following an artistic direction, yet that direction was still unclear. But by 1972 prog had already delivered three solid gold classic albums: Yes' *Close To The Edge*, King Crimson's *In The Court Of The Crimson King* and Genesis' *Foxtrot*, with the first and third of those three LPs boasting, like *Meddle*, one side-long epic of trailblazing quality. Pink Floyd, meanwhile, though they had maintained a high overall standard and delivered a number of inspired recordings, still struggled somewhat in the backwaters. For all the exceptional quality of *Echoes*, side one of the album it graced was an uneasy mix of quirky, strange and unsuccessful. It did not compare with *Close To The Edge*.

After *Echoes*, Roger Waters in particular felt the urge to expand his creative horizons. With progressive rock in full flow and already glittering with classics, the time was ripe for Pink Floyd to stretch themselves and deliver something of equivalent quality. *Echoes* became the pivot around which the group turned. That song was complex, beautiful, sophisticated and lengthy. It was the template of the future. There would be no howling dogs on the new album, no folky oddities, no longueurs. The group was going to aim their music directly at the heart of humanity.

For *The Dark Side Of The Moon*, Waters assumed the position of sole lyricist. His theme was the human condition itself, as revealed to himself and the group as they lived their music biz lives. That choice formed a deep, broad channel, along which the music would flow like an unstoppable river, carrying listeners along on a sonic journey the like of which they had rarely, if ever, experienced before. And lyrics were important to prog groups. Lyrical concerns, rejecting the whimsical or trivial, or the adolescent love-based couplets of mere pop bands, were elevated. It had long been observed that Jon Anderson's lyrics were only semi-comprehensible, but they had a remarkable poesy about them, making them fascinating, if sometimes opaque. Anderson, when he spoke of love, did so from an academic or spiritual position more often than not. He used the *sounds* of words as much as creating meaning with them. King Crimson, meanwhile, had already written *21st Century Schizoid Man*, which even today resonates with power and subtle influence, and which at the beginning of the prog rock boom sounded like nothing else on the planet. Prog rock lyrics, then, were crucial; they tended towards wise, profound, to elsewhere and elsewhen. They had to raise the listener intellectually as well as enthral them.

Waters found himself trawling many sources. A young man whose family background had inculcated within him a certain amount of bitter horror at the world, some of those sources were personal. He wrote of the madness of war, of its imbalanced social hierarchy; and he wrote of madness itself. He wrote about times of death and destruction; and of time itself. He wrote about money; football teams and the root of all evil. This was set according to the group's understated manner, which both manifested and epitomised their perfectly English backgrounds. The lyrics of the six main songs were a summary of life according to a man of Waters' era: post-war, infiltrated by American economics and culture, baffled by ennui, perplexed by the relentless passing of weeks, months and years. Time's arrow led only to death.

Six of the nine main pieces were songs with lyrics. The other three were instrumentals, one of which, *The Great Gig In The Sky*, was uncategorisable.

The opening of the album invokes the beginning of life. A heartbeat: perpetual, subtle. Over that vital indicator of human existence flutter dreamlike impressions of parts of the album, including the cash register on *Money*, the ticking clock of *Time*, and a fragment of Clare Torry's impassioned vocal. Two voices speak of madness. At just over a minute, it is a *musique concréte* overture to the main show; a pre-hallucination.

At the seamless change into *Breathe (In The Air)*, a backwards piano rises up, segueing into the first song. Sung with languorous ease by Gilmour, the song evokes the simple yet profound verities of living in its opening line, from which the song's title is taken, yet almost at once injects a note of concern, suggesting to the listener that caring is a perilous art of which they must not be afraid. This undercurrent of unease continues as the lyrics evoke the sensual side of life – smiling, touching, seeing, crying – with an emotional depth that comes in part from its simple form. But simplicity is often paired with such concerns. The sense of perturbation is enhanced with the 'Run, rabbit run,' image; a hint of pursuit, a hint of the relentlessness of a life digging holes, and perhaps a hint of war via this opening lyric from another song. The final line, however, is unequivocal: an early death is on the cards for some. Waters here reaches out into traditional, tedious life in his search for meaning, his lyrics already ambiguous, sinister and ominous.

On *Time,* the lyrical concerns are similar, but with a much more urgent tenor. Now the listener is wasting their time, day by day, hour by hour, on trivialities and diversions. Meaninglessness in middle-class Western life is evoked by the image of somebody hanging around, perhaps hands in pockets, waiting for the meaning of life to be provided; though not by themselves, by somebody else. It is an image that many listeners place into their own boring, repetitive, unfulfilling lives; on street corners, in parks too small to expand into, without rhyme or reason, in an urban labyrinth created too far in the past to make sense to disaffected youth. People seek the meaning of life but are too afraid, too locked-in, too scared of death and too frightened of standing up to make their mark. The nail which stands out is the one hammered down, as the old saying has it. And in the latter half of the song, it is old age which is the harbinger of death. (As Gilmour had it in one of his solo songs later on, this is about wondering if you're getting older and wiser, when you're just getting old.) The song features one of Waters' greatest lines: *Hanging on in quiet desperation is the English way.* A reprise of *Breathe* gives a more personal, but also gut-wrenching, interpretation of time and life. There is a log fire for an old man at home; a wide field and something like peace, before the sound of a bell, and the knowledge of faithful observers nearby kneeling at prayer…

The Great Gig In The Sky is founded on a Wright chord sequence, its recording essentially one of ambition and good luck. For this track, a young vocalist of engineer Alan Parsons' acquaintance was brought into the studio. Her name was Clare Torry, and at first she was unsure what the group wanted. But in due course, these unassuming English gentlemen got across what they wanted, and – first take – Torry provided. Her vocal was mostly improvised, and at the time few people realised the impact of those brief minutes. Yet her vocal added another layer to the legendary status of this album. Once again, something of true greatness had been wrested from chance and the group's musicality.

The second side kicks off with a dissection of the influence of money. Although *Money* is satirised as sixth-form poetry by Waters around the turn of the decade in one of his own pieces, it stands nonetheless as a succinct, well-observed paean to the unwholesome power of filthy lucre. As far back as 1973 he was invoking the purchase of football teams as an indicator of the wasteful, pointless use of cash in the service of self-interest; enlightened self-interest, as capitalists have it. That ethos is all about cars and caviar, the Learjet life in the jet set age. The lyrics lay bare the temptation of feathering your own nest at the expense of others; and talking about charitable donation is just bullshit. Well, yes – and it still is, as those who view "billionaire philanthropists" with a cynical gaze know only too well.

From the root of all evil, Waters turns to the inhumanity of war in *Us & Them*, with its social separation into commoner soldiers and privileged officers, a perverted hierarchy warping the entire war-strewn twentieth century. This song strikes out at the core insanity of war, yet in poetic terms is allusive rather than vivid, subtle horror, not gore-splattered. Waters' images are removed from the gun-and-bayonet truth of the battlefield. They are concerned with the ubiquity of warfare, in overarching, almost wistful, yet somehow disturbing terms. Up and down… side to side… down and out… these strange, semi-formed lines, as they seem, disorient the listener via their subtle intent. It is a kind of awful preliminary to full-blown madness.

The penultimate song *Brain Damage* is about madness, taking its cue from the implied dysfunction of the album's title. The moon is source and regulator: our moon, the loon, lunatic, lunacy, lunatics in the loony bin. It is social dysfunction and personal dysfunction all in one, with some loonies outdoors on the lawn and pictured in newspapers, but others appearing in the world of the song's viewpoint character – in their own front hall, no less. And at length, such day-to-day lunacy is internal, in the head, disrupting thoughts, intrusive, lobotomy, a padded cell in the local loony bin, where somebody weird and unknown resides… very much *not* the person born at the beginning of the album in a sentient pitter-patter of heartbeats. Through these lyrics, the listener becomes a stranger to themself.

Eclipse provides the finale in a cosmic detonation of three-word and four-word lines, each a tiny nugget blowing up the sensory experiences of life – smiling, touching, seeing, crying, tasting, feeling – before moving on to explode the deeper verities of life – loving, hating, distrusting, saving, buying, begging, borrowing and stealing. In this bonfire of the sanities, even creation and destruction bow before the implacable, irreversible power of sun and moon. For the sun measures out our three score years and ten, while the moon blots out our deepest secrets and worst excesses, our battles and love affairs, even our very words… even *these* words, which will in time be annihilated as our expanding scarlet sun turns earth and moon to ash.

Life seems meaningless to so many, yet meaning is our core: the heart of the human condition. It is around that truth that *The Dark Side Of The Moon* wraps its limbs. It takes both our ephemera and our deepest desires and turns them into a musical visitation, as if by human exemplars from the far future. Newspaper voyeurism and the inevitability of death are compounded into forty-two minutes and fifty seconds; helicopters and a chase scene, the simple pleasures of life and the deepest yearnings. It is all there.

The Dark Side Of The Moon was an album that prioritised the voice, but not just through Gilmour, Wright and Waters taking vocal parts, as they had on previous albums, either singing as lead vocalist, or, in the case of Gilmour and Wright, singing often with the other providing a harmony. There was a brand new, not to mention unexpected, addition: female backing vocals. These vocals manifested something never before found on a Pink Floyd album: soul. The vocals, provided by Leslie Duncan, Barry St John, Liza Strike and Doris Troy, had a distinctly American feel to them and were used throughout the album, notably on *Time* and *Us & Them*. To the monumental feel of both of these tracks, with their lyrics speaking of passing time, especially at the end of human lives, and of the madness of war, a new sound was added, this choir of soulful voices, which broadened the vocal range and depth of the singing into something of awe-inspiring impact. Vibrato and Stateside soul vocal techniques gave emotional impact to the massed ranks of voices, with Gilmour's voice on *Time* somehow grasped, raised and transported into a sonic empyrean, filled with transcendent possibilities. He was not just David

Gilmour and Wright was not just Richard Wright when they sang this song, the two were part of a sacred interplay of voices; their own, masculine yet soft, English and cultured, and never more than restrained, counterpoised by the quartet of vibrato-rich, transatlantic, soulful voices, which not only balanced the genders, but also the emotional content and even the cultural origins. That mix of American and English origins broadened not only the appeal of the music – the album was the group's first huge hit in the States – but gave the songs extra cultural diversity, turning something already full of wisdom and wonder into something sublime.

The four members of the group were typical Englishmen in one regard: their restraint, their capacity for understatement, their quietness, and their studious air, as of young men recently emerged from some national establishment of modesty. Quiet speech is the English way. Modest manners were their trademark, spoken in the most subtle form of received pronunciation. Yet to this epitome of Englishness was coupled the wild, vibrato-heavy, emotive vocals of the backing quartet, a pairing which on paper should not have worked, yet, because of the universality of the lyrics' themes, the brilliance of the arrangements and mixing, and the musicianship of the group, became far more than the sum of its parts.

A further use of the human voice to maximise emotional impact was employed at the end of the first side, in one of the most legendary rock recordings ever. It would have been easy for the group to have written a song about death, using one of Wright's chord sequences, and with witty, insightful lyrics courtesy of Waters; and that would have created a great song. But something more was required for this album, in which the human voice gave form to emotional content and universal themes.

Without words, using just wails, oohs and aahs, and a few soulful vocal techniques, Clare Torry evoked the tragedy of death, its inevitability, the impact it has on those left behind, beginning with the tragedy and inevitability, then, in a quieter section, evoking sorrow, again using marvellous, emotive wordless singing that said so much more than any Waters couplet could. Moreover, the chord sequence – left over from Wright's earlier offerings – was original enough to give Torry the chance to respond in melody as well as sheer vocal prowess, as during a classic Wright key change towards the end. Her descending vocal runs at the track's conclusion evoked in stark form what is left after death: just people, standing together, sometimes still isolated, sometimes in union. It was all there, performed without words, without input from the group's lyricist, indeed without anything standing as an obstacle between the listener and those breathtaking sounds of the human voice. It was proof, if proof were needed, that human beings do not necessarily need words to communicate, and that, in certain circumstances, emotion does it better.

Even away from the singers and vocalists of this album, there was a further development that allowed human vocal possibilities to come to the fore. Another first for the group was the use of the saxophone. This instrument, though typically used in jazz and traditional rock music, can lay claim to being the instrument most akin in tonal range and emotive possibilities to the human voice. It is often described in such terms. When the group used a raucous saxophone on *Money* and a more laid-back, contemplative saxophone on the following cut, they were adding yet another human voice to the mix, though no voice was used. The sax took that part. In free-wheeling, gutsy, honking tones on *Money,* the saxophone became an arrogant financial dealer rolling in lovely loot, a rich man so proud of his hi-fi. The slapback echo somehow defined the arena in which all that money was made and enjoyed: small, private, restricted, probably on the south coast of France, probably with a successful football team. The sound was guttural, full of phlegm, and boxy, yet that box was for men of finance and wealth their playground of the world.

For *Us & Them,* an entirely different voice was required. Evoking the madness and pain of war, this saxophone needed to be soft; breathy, yes, but in an altogether calmer mode. But it also needed to rise above the fray, evoking comradeship and courage as well as death and despair. The sound was smooth, rougher occasionally, but even as it rose and emoted somehow a voice of stately dignity. It was a voice of compassion as well as calamity, paralleling Gilmour's voice, supporting it, yet also evoking those martial emotions Gilmour did not. Gilmour and the saxophone were a fused dyad, one using words and subtle dignity, the other evoking all the intense feelings of any band of brothers.

Three other vocal augmentations marked the album. Spoken voices floated in and out of the music, commenting in natural speech on topics like death, madness and violence. Although the technique had been tried before, *The*

Dark Side Of The Moon was the first rock album to integrate speech in such an original and effective way. There were voices, too, at the end of *On The Run:* distorted, unearthly voices, laughing at the insignificant human they were chasing. Or perhaps they were robots of the machine, built by human beings and trying to overcome them. A third voice was David Gilmour's, not singing but used alongside his bluesy solo on *Any Colour You Like,* echoing it. This voice was more apparent when the group played live, but made a subtle and spine-tingling addition to an already marvellous solo.

This was the group's album of the voice, then. They had explored their voices before, and even used a choir on an earlier album, but for *The Dark Side Of The Moon,* they used every vocal technique possible to connect the listener with their own emotions and the burgeoning emotions of the group. This melding of a multitude of human voices was a foundation of the LP's success.

But there was one other factor, something not grasped often enough by modern students of music. This was 1973, just six years after *Sgt. Pepper's Lonely Hearts Club Band,* and just three years after the end of the 1960s. In that decade, as in the following one, what mattered in pop and rock music was *melody.*

Melody is music's path into human emotion. A rock song with little or no melody, which nevertheless has brilliant lyrics, can be appreciated as a work of poetry. Any song, however, which carries its lyrics on wings of melody is poised to *move* listeners, to make them *feel* something, to have an *emotional* impact.

Every one of the songs on *The Dark Side Of The Moon* was a miniature miracle of melody, from the balmy tune of *Breathe* through the epic melody of *Us & Them* all the way to the simple yet majestic tune concluding the album. Even the instrumental *Any Colour You Like* featured a highly melodic synth solo from Wright, and a guitar solo full of tuneful interplay. And so, because of the melodic heart of these compositions, their finely crafted lyrics were catapulted into an arena that almost all listeners, English, American or global, could grasp, empathise with, love and cherish. This was not just a superb progressive rock album; it was one of those rarest of entities, an album of timeless appeal and universal accessibility.

Such albums come along once per decade, if we are lucky. And so often they are firsts. *Sgt. Pepper's Lonely Hearts Club Band* derives much of its unique brilliance from the fact that The Beatles were striking out into the territory for the first time, as themselves, but also as representatives of rock music. For all *Revolver*'s differences when compared with previous Beatles albums, it was still an album of rock songs, presented in the usual format with pretty much the usual instruments. Brilliant, yes; unforgettable, in fact. 1967's masterpiece however, was not only a concept album, it used radically different instruments and arrangements. This was a qualitative difference; a true break from the past. Thus, *Sgt. Pepper's Lonely Hearts Club Band* was a first, not only for the band but for music as a whole. It discovered and opened up territory nobody had known existed before. *The Dark Side Of The Moon* occupied the same place, but in the field of progressive rock. It was akin to *Sgt Pepper* because it was a first – for the group, who were reaching out from their English, stylised, often psychedelic origins to a place where they explored their own emotions and some universal human themes, and for music, for which an album that not only fused melody, voice, emotion and insight, but which ran as two seamless sides, was a mind-blowing innovation. Even The Beatles separated most of the songs on their album with gaps. Pink Floyd merged everything into a sonic experience unmatched at the time.

This is why the album was timeless, and why it had such critical and commercial success. Almost everyone could relate to it. It spoke to everybody, through its melodies, its lyrics, and through its groundbreaking use of voices and instruments akin to voices.

Then there was the music itself.

Pink Floyd were not masters of technique, at least, not in the prog sense. They certainly were masters. But Gilmour's languid, bluesy guitar technique, in which almost every note was bent, was conspicuously less showy than, say, John McLaughlin's, who could play notes so fast they blurred into a sonic fluid, just as individual pictures at twenty-five frames per second blur into film motion. Wright, meanwhile, was no Keith Emerson. He insisted on using his fingers, not knives. He was, to use his own expression, a jazzer. But with Mason at the drums and Waters providing a solid, if uneventful bass, the quartet became that most magical of musical entities: more than the sum of their parts. And they were keen to progress. All four were progressive. Their youthful but imaginative engineer, Alan Parsons, was also progressive.

Following the impressionistic intro composed of sonic shards and the first song proper came something which truly was groundbreaking. *On The Run* was an instrumental evoking, in breathtaking stereo and at hi-fi quality, a thrilling chase, with the listener, represented by their pattering footfall, pursued by some variety of behemoth, evoked by massive synth blocks and an urgent, mutating, ever-oscillating ostinato. The piece was originally called *The Travel Sequence,* recalling Wright's fear of death during extended group travel. Shortly before a recording session, the group had taken delivery of a very early synthesiser, the EMS Synthi AKS, which Gilmour one day found himself playing with, specifically the sequencer. He and Waters soon found that by adding a white noise hi-hat sound and speeding the sequence up, they created an eerie ostinato, the timbre of which could be altered with resonance and cut off controls; in the take appearing on the album, that was Gilmour's work. But this synth was an early adventure into electronics, so the sequence had to be input every time it was required. (I remember making my own first foray into EMS-based electronic music in 1980, and can confirm that the primitive quality of the synthesiser was at once fascinating and infuriating.)

Soon enough, a marvellous pattering track emerged based around Waters' eight notes, over which the group and Parsons stacked immense sounds, and noises more enigmatic – voices, perhaps, of robots, or even aliens. All this sonic magic evoked aeroplane flight and travel in general, with the latter part of the track imagining via *audio verité* a terrifying chase enacted between a tiny human being and gargantuan machines, which, as they swooped across the stereo spectrum, even had their sound shifted by the Doppler effect.

This track cohered as 1972 segued into 1973. For context, at this time those peerless masters of the synthesiser Tangerine Dream had only recently acquired a Moog synth, and were themselves a year away from their own groundbreaking electronic music, of which *On The Run* turned out to be a prescient forerunner. In 1972, Tangerine Dream released the icy, spacious *Zeit,* with 1973's *Atem* as yet nascent. The group's groundbreaking *Phaedra* was a non-conceived entity when Gilmour and Waters were playing with their new toy. *On The Run* really was a trailblazer – a flight into the unknown powered by chance and outstanding musicality.

Meanwhile, Wright's keyboards and synthesisers had never sounded so good. On *Any Colour You Like,* his EMS VCS3 was fed into a lengthy tape loop, so that the melodic part he played decayed and ascended, giving a superlative spacious quality to the sound. The drums clattered and hissed underneath, driving the track, alongside which other keyboards thrummed. This wordless piece evoked forward motion, spirals, dives and glides, and wide open air inside huge spaces. It was a propulsive instrumental serving as a counterpoint to the suspenseful *On The Run,* with its claustrophobia and fear, all of which were sublimated or dismissed as its free-flowing music sped on. *Any Colour You Like* was motion conveyed by music: awesome, liberating, free and expansive.

Gilmour's solo on the track also conveyed motion, but via emotion. Feeding harmonised guitars into a Uni-Vibe phase-shifter and adding complementary vocals created a much fuller sound than just one instrument taking a solo. It was a chorus of guitars, the voice bringing an emotive vibe to the solo.

The Dark Side Of The Moon benefited from two additional factors, one deliberate, one accidental. The former was the engagement of Alan Parsons as producer. Parsons would go on to make a significant contribution to the world of rock music in his own right as the head of The Alan Parsons Project, a group (using the word loosely) which fused rock smarts with pop melodies, and which became unaccountably successful in America. At the time, however, he was only known inside the tiny world of professional recording. Parsons functioned, sometimes deliberately, sometimes accidentally, as the producer of the album. It was he who took his tape machine and microphone to a nearby clock shop to make the recordings which would, in due course, and with such thrilling intensity, announce the beginning of the track *Time.* Parsons also brought in Clare Torry, to sing over Wright's melancholic chord sequence with devastating effect.

The accidental factor was the presence of Chris Thomas, brought in to mix the album once it was finished. His instinct was to make more of the link passages and snatches of speech and other sounds which gave the album such extraordinary verity. Waters' lyrics were superior to many others, evoking with concise candour the trials, mistakes and subsequent disillusionment of the typical human being. The group's music carried these thoughts and concepts to perfection. But what made this album qualitatively different – in

Cambridge city centre. (*Public domain*)

Arnold Layne 45 single, 10 March 1967. (*Hal Harries*)

See Emily Play 45 single, 16 June 1967. (*Hal Harries*)

Photograph of *Hit Parader* magazine Pink Floyd image, 1968. (*Public domain*)

The Little Grey Men by B.B., 1967 copy owned by the author. (*Author's collection*)

Abbey Road recording studios. (*Public domain*)

Syd Barrett's Fender Esquire mirrored guitar. (*Public domain*)

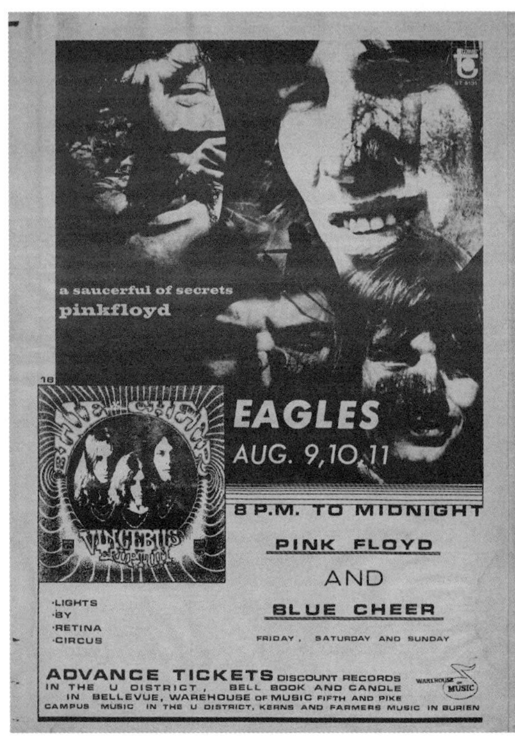

US *Helix* magazine concert advertisement from 1968. (*Public domain*)

Magazine cutting from 1969. (*Public domain*)

Billboard magazine cutting from 1971. (*Public domain*)

Pompeii ruins. (*Jo Lashly*)

The Dark Side Of The Moon prism image planetarium. (*Frank Schwichtenberg, GNU Free Documentation License*)

The author and the central *Wish You Were Here* image at HMV in Exeter. (*Author's collection*)

Battersea Power Station. (*Public domain*)

Raving & Drooling LP bootleg from 1976. (*Jon Champignon*)

Raving & Drooling LP bootleg cover. (*Jon Champignon*)

Another Brick In The Wall single. (*Public domain*)

The City Of London Academy, Islington, from where pupils sang on *Another Brick In The Wall*. (*Public domain*)

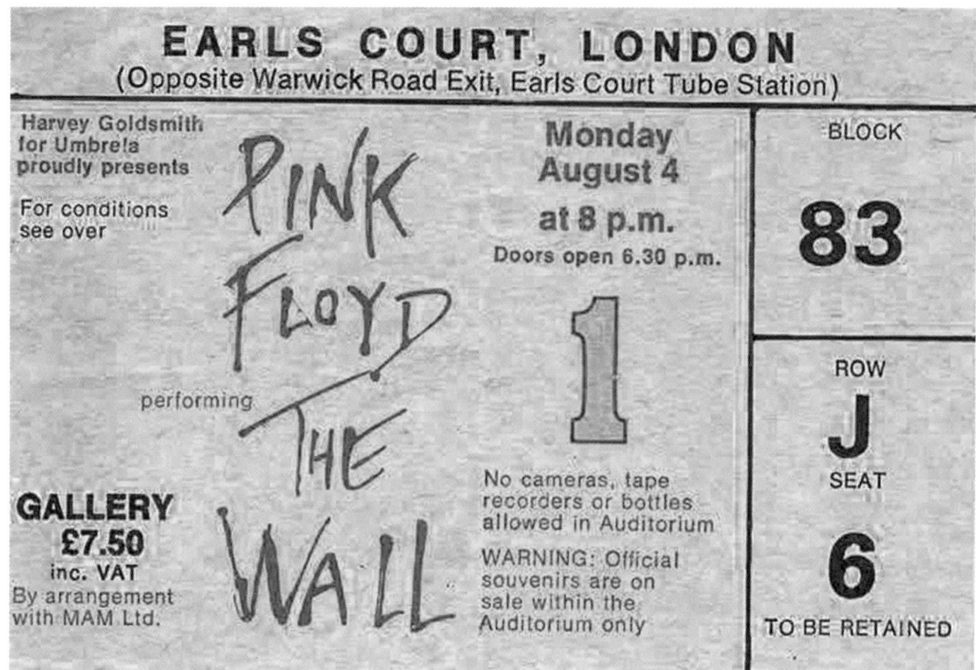

The Wall live ticket, 4 August 1980 at Earls Court. (*Oz Hardwick*)

The Wall live concert, Earls Court, wall and smoke. (*TITCH*)

The Wall live concert, Earls Court, flying pig. (*TITCH*)

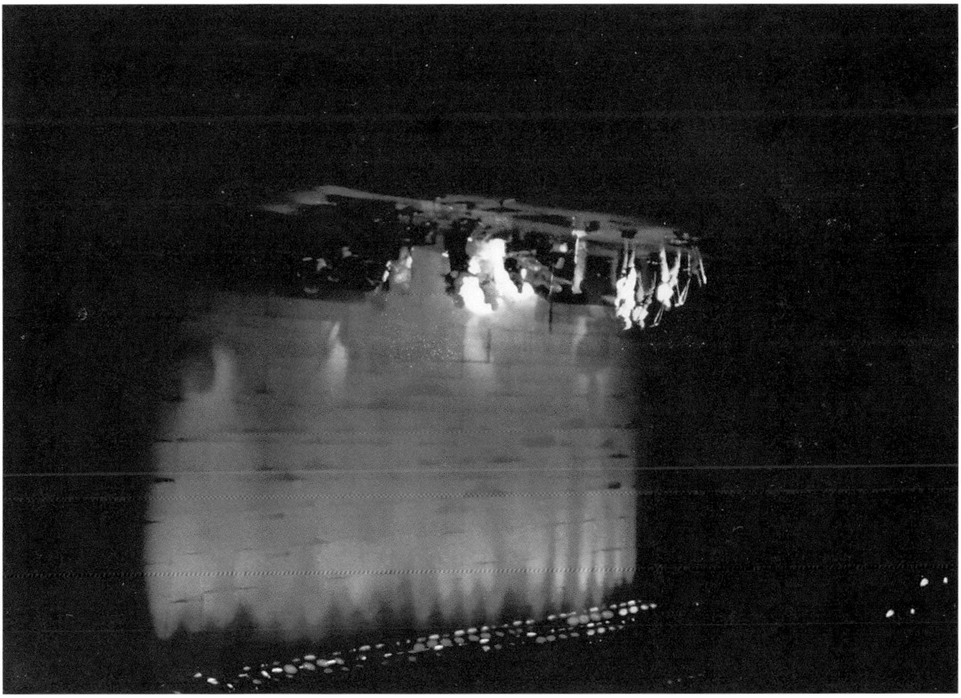

The Wall live concert, Earls Court, full wall. (*TITCH*)

The Wall live concert, Earls Court, falling wall. (*TITCH*)

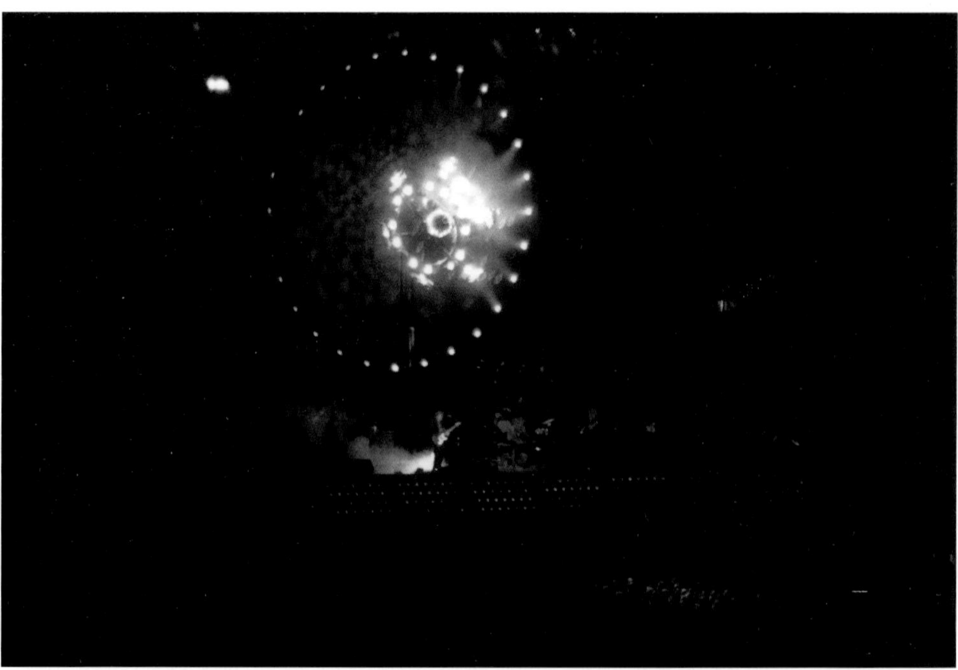

Pink Floyd's A *Momentary Lapse of Reason* tour, Toronto, 1987. (*Wikimedia Creative Commons*)

Pink Floyd 3 December 1987 *A Momentary Lapse Of Reason* tour ticket. (*Edzep11*)

Pink Floyd 1 August 1988 tour ticket, rescheduled to 8 August. (*Alan Busby*)

1994 CD Italian-sourced bootleg album owned by the author. (*Author's collection*)

Roger Waters 10 June 2023 in Manchester, with Syd Barrett projected. (*Oz Hardwick*)

Roger Waters 10 June 2023 in Manchester, flying pig. (*Oz Hardwick*)

Nick Mason's Saucerful Of Secrets tour 12 June 2024 in York, full band. (*Oz Hardwick*)

Nick Mason's Saucerful Of Secrets tour 16 April 2022 in York, Nick Mason. (*Oz Hardwick*)

Nick Mason's Saucerful Of Secrets tour 16 April 2022 in York, gong. (*Oz Hardwick*)

effect one of the first LPs which *had* to be listened to in its entirety – was Thomas' mixing in of those voices, now so familiar to fans, those footsteps tapping on the wooden floor of the group's Abbey Road studio, those clocks, those forebodings of the *Great Gig In The Sky*, that vocoder-like laughter akin to aliens mocking humanity. All this gave the album its deeper truth.

The group made an album evoking the inner world of millions of human beings. It was in effect an expression of theatre, velvet and intense, hypnotic and intoxicating. Because this album was founded on questions *everybody* has to face, and sometimes even answer, it achieved a commercial reach that took it to the summit of its potential. Inner worlds had been explored before, but not on this scale, without the dramatic intent, and using less compelling music.

To listen to *The Dark Side Of The Moon* was to be immersed in a drama, presented in an apparently innocuous format, yet which had the power to conjure images, sensations, feelings and emotions which underscored and magnified the deepest qualities of the human condition. That theatre of the imagination, conveyed via headphones or hi-fi speakers, stood for innumerable personal experiences, which every single listener already knew. It was this merging of the human universal, the lyrical and the musical which made such a deep impression upon millions of listeners. Such achievements happen only occasionally in our lifetimes.

These, then, were the components of the album. Pink Floyd were artists, and at last all their creative exploration and experimentation had cohered into something of transcendent beauty. Gilmour recalled later in a radio interview that the first time they all sat together in the studio to listen to a run-through, they realised they had recorded something special. But the components were not the end of the matter. Pink Floyd's components combined into something impossible to predict even during recording. There was an additional factor.

This was a concept album, but that was not a new phenomenon. *Sgt. Pepper's Lonely Hearts Club Band* was the first such release, an LP which even now has a claim to being the greatest of them all. And there had been others in the meantime. *The Dark Side Of The Moon* had as its concept the human condition itself, as filtered by the group through their own experiences, but it was not a collection of songs as per The Beatles' masterpiece. This LP was a single, whole, nonpareil entity that could only be appreciated in its entirety. If LPs only had one side, there would likely have been no break between *The Great Gig In The Sky* and *Money*. True, *Sgt Pepper* was best experienced in its entirety, but the songs were separate and could be enjoyed as perfect vignettes of the band. The songs on *The Dark Side Of The Moon* divulged their full meaning when listened to in the context of the album. A single taken off the LP only appeared in America, and then for commercial reasons alone. No such thing happened in the country that nurtured the group. Indeed, that idea was deemed rather crass and pointless by some there – nobody needed to photograph one corner of Picasso's *Guernica* in order to promote it. That painting was an inviolate creation. As was this Pink Floyd album.

I first heard *The Dark Side Of The Moon* on a cassette, listening with primitive headphones late at night in bed at home. It was a transformative experience for me – fifteen at the time and discovering the joys of progressive and electronic music. As the years went by and my teens slipped into my twenties and then thirties, I noticed something peculiar. When deciding what album to listen to, I felt a disinclination to put *The Dark Side Of The Moon* on. For a while, that bothered and baffled me, but now I know what it was that I felt. I got to know the album so well, and love it so much, that repeated plays became a meaningless experience. That specialness a music-lover feels when discovering some wonderful new group or revisiting a treasured LP is *diminished* by listening too often. Something special and full of meaning becomes something mundane, so all true music-lovers instinctively shy away from this. They put the album back and choose something else. Having created their own meaning in the assimilation and understanding of the album, both through their own emotional response and through the context in which the album appeared, they do not wish to sully that response by over-exposure. For that is what happens. If I listened to Pink Floyd's masterpiece over and over again, I would taint it, spoil it, in acts which for me would be a disgrace.

I don't feel like this only about *The Dark Side Of The Moon*, I feel it about *Rubycon, Relayer, Hergest Ridge*, Klaus Schulze's "*X*" and Steve Reich's *Music For 18 Musicians*. These are works of deep meaning to me, which have become part of my identity. All who love music make their own personal relationships with musical greatness, especially during their teens and twenties, and everyone who listens to *The Dark Side Of The Moon* and loves it knows it is something special. Perhaps such feelings will become less common and more eccentric, when they exist at all, as technology and new culture move the tides of music into new territory. But listening to this album in its entirety and in the correct order, as the group intended, is surely the only way to appreciate just what an extraordinary work it is. Indeed, it is not "just" an album. It is a node in interconnected musical culture, an exemplar and an inspiration, something which brings people together through its exploration of shared humanity. It does not do this through its lyrics, nor through its music. *Both* aspects contribute to this magical creation. The experiences it generates are both deeply personal and universal. And that is a rare thing.

Chapter 11

Wish You Were Here

Following up on a masterpiece is never easy. The word itself comes from the days when a craftsperson was about to cross the boundary between apprentice, albeit skilled, and master. A masterpiece would be their one-off work, intended to declare once and for all that the individual was indeed a master. Such works were judged by other masters. The existence of one masterpiece implied was that there could be others, yet that was never guaranteed. Creative work, after all, exists in a cultural and social context, and such media may change. Tastes may alter, external ideas may upend tradition, and there is always the possibility of a paradigm change.

The four men of Pink Floyd knew they had created a masterpiece with *The Dark Side Of The Moon*. When they heard the playback for the first time, they knew it was special. What was unexpected was the commercial and cultural impact. No musician expects to give birth to a behemoth, still less one so gorgeous and almost universally admired. The Beatles in 1967, basking in the warmth of being the first explorers of virgin rock territory, and aware that the flawless *Sgt. Pepper's Lonely Hearts Club Band* was a groundbreaking LP never to be repeated, struggled to follow it up. *Magical Mystery Tour* had the usual array of unique, melodious songs, but it re-trod the same ground; never a good look. Months later, they decided to revert to earlier styles and influences, producing *The White Album*. But even by 1968, the legacy of *Sgt Pepper* was assured. Nobody could listen to it and not have their breath taken away. It stands forever as a testament to genius, a summit from which the only path is downhill.

For Pink Floyd, aware as early as 1974 that something special was fast expanding into the public awareness, the problem was as acute as that facing The Beatles. It could be argued that Pink Floyd had to face making a follow-up to two masterpieces, but the impact of *The Piper At The Gates Of Dawn* was only felt in distant retrospect, although it was admired and adored upon release. That album was more Syd Barrett's masterpiece anyway. Yet the difficulty of the group's situation was evinced more by *Ummagumma* than by *A Saucerful Of Secrets,* which bridged two musical worlds. And *Ummagumma* was a mess. *The White Album* was not a mess, but it was a diamond with a flaw.

Pink Floyd, therefore, faced a musical dilemma. How could they possibly follow a trailblazing LP such as *The Dark Side Of The Moon?* How could they recapture that astonishing creative leap? Could they create a second work of equal brilliance? *Should* they?

Used to working up musical ideas while on tour, the group found themselves floundering again. There was no inspirational fuel in the tank. The view post-masterpiece was of many downhill paths. Roger Waters, now established through *Echoes* and *The Dark Side Of The Moon* as the man who made the concepts, was stuck for ideas. Worse, the music press noticed this, and began hinting that Pink Floyd was a spent force.

For a while, the group toyed with the most radical ideas available. Observing that their masterpiece oozed flawless musical quality, they tried renouncing all such notions, pondering a concept with the working title of *Household Objects,* in which the music would be made by non-musical instruments. This was true to their art group roots, but, as a practical method, it lacked plausibility. It would be like painting with tree branches after the Mona Lisa. Soon they returned to the tried and tested format of guitar, bass, keyboards and drums.

Then, one day in the studio, bathing in unspoken ennui, David Gilmour found himself playing his guitar. Roger Waters sat nearby. Without warning, four notes fell out of Gilmour's strings: two pairs of ascending notes. *B-flat, F, G, E...*

Something in that haunting, simple, elegiac theme caught Waters' ears. It reminded him of all that the group had lost since their psychedelic days, now almost a decade in the past. The guiding hand of Barrett, the group's songwriter; the colourful garments of the Summer of Love; the hope and optimism of 1967; the proximity of the Beatles and the dawn of the rock LP. But it was Syd Barrett that Waters missed most, his partner in the earliest days, before the name Pink Floyd was coined, when they were naive architecture students in swinging London. The 1974/5 dilemma of the group, sitting in the studio, drinking wine and glancing at one another in the English way, matched the 1967/8 dilemma, in which Syd's glorious songs, which he alone could write, were gone forever. They had some material, but, somehow, the days of 1973 had also disappeared into unfathomable retrospect, and the material lacked context. *The Dark Side Of The Moon* was, of course, unrepeatable. Waters sensed this, grasping also that in one sense the band should not really bother continuing. But what else could they do? They were Pink Floyd. A responsibility fell upon their shoulders, now creaking and groaning under the weight of that trailblazing LP. Thinking of his childhood friend, and listening to the four notes played by Gilmour, Waters suddenly got in touch with the huge gap left by the tragic departure of Barrett, taken, perhaps in a single weekend, by the many drugs of the past. His feelings were about regret, passing, loss, absence. He wished Barrett were here.

Though they had lost that sorcerous element of melody and verbal whimsy manifested by Barrett, the group had proved themselves capable of writing powerful, stirring, beautiful music. Rick Wright was a master of melody. Roger Waters, though fuelled by a lyrical spirit diametrically opposed to Barrett's, could craft a couplet like few others. Gilmour was an exceptional guitarist and vocalist, and composer. Mason was the rhythmic foundation of it all. So it was that in Waters' mind a new concept began to arise. His feelings, stirred by Gilmour's enigmatic quartet of notes, were strong enough to support an LP concept. The situation of the group matched their situation in 1968-69, and after a period of drifting and false starts, they at last had a framework for the new music that was emerging.

Soon, the grand concepts that had supported and enveloped their music since *Echoes* had a new sibling. The new LP would begin and finish with a lengthy ode to the situation the group found themselves in. Through the agency of their stately music, Wright's increasing use of synthesisers as opposed to traditional keyboards, and Waters' melancholy regret at the absence of Syd Barrett, a piece entitled *Shine On You Crazy Diamond* emerged. It was slow, serene, mournful and beautiful. The first side of the LP would be dominated by it, while the second side would conclude with it. In between, other songs were fixed, all of them brewed in discontent, sharp observation, and classic English emotional understatement. The group, which could have packed it all in after their masterpiece, were finding out what it was like to carry on. Each of their creative minds were synchronised once again with their bodies, and with the other three minds comprising the group.

For an album released in 1975, *Wish You Were Here* began with a daring opening, which in its own way also broke new ground. For some time, a solitary G minor chord drifted into view: nothing more, not demanding, with no rhythm or vocal or solo. It prefigured the ambient music that, at the time, Brian Eno was beginning to conceive, and which, almost two decades later, would for a while become an emerging phenomenon in British music. But in 1975, it was verging on revolutionary. Rick Wright created it using a string synthesiser and other keyboards, while in the final mix, a recycled part created on a wine glass harp from *Household Objects* was used. After this keyboard section – which seemed to hover in the listener's awareness like the thrum of a gossamer spaceship – one of David Gilmour's most lyrical guitar solos began, in which the beauty of his string-bending technique was perhaps best displayed. No other guitarist could have written and played it. His style, fomented in the hurly-burly of the 1960s and honed at the turn of the decade, was now as unique as all the other great masters of the rock guitar. His sound was unmistakable, and he existed in the same pantheon as Beck and Page and Howe and Hillage. Every black Fender apprentice wanted to worship at this deity's feet.

After this solo came the inspirational four-note guitar part created by Gilmour, which at once enfolded the mood of the previous music and gave it a much sharper edge. Any listener hearing it for the first time knew something was about to happen. Those four notes at once warned of the emotional impact to come and set it up, as the whole group, founded on Mason's brilliant rhythmic propulsion, sprang into full band mode. The tempo was stately and the mood minor, but Pink Floyd were on the move once again. Amidst all this, Gilmour continued his six-string exploration of the mood of elegy and absence.

Echoes and *The Dark Side Of The Moon* had featured Gilmour and Wright as main vocalists, with Waters little in evidence, but it was entirely fitting that he should sing the words for *Shine On You Crazy Diamond*. Moreover, this was not so much of an emotionally distant lyric; it was: *Remember when we were young…* and that *we* was clearly Waters and Barrett, with the rest of the group included by implication. This was *personal*. Waters sang of a man not present, a creative one-off, the heart of the original group, albeit surrounded by great talent, and the resident songwriter, too. Waters' lyrics were all about *we* and *you*. Though earlier songs had arrived with considerable emotional impact, their verbal form tended to be more from an omniscient perspective: descriptive, allusive, metaphorical, evocative. There was a didactic element, a sense of observation from a distance: don't be afraid to care… all you distrust… all you save… But *Shine On You Crazy Diamond* launches straight into the heart of the matter. It is one man speaking to one absent other: subjective, heartfelt. Do you remember when we were young? Do you remember me coming over to your house and listening to you play guitar? You were two years younger than us, do you recall Regent Street? We were architecture students. Then we got into music and found ourselves in the centre of Swinging London. Do you remember all that? Amidst all that psychedelic colour and explosive social change, you shone as bright as the sun.

The chorus is augmented by extra voices (Venetta Fields and Carlena Williams), and by a baritone saxophone solo that floats in over more staccato music: Dick Parry once more. As the music changes rhythmic structure, Parry moves from his mournful deeper sax to one that flies through this changed musical sky, a whirling tenor amidst guitar arpeggios and the rest of the band. Then the music fades, part one, side one over.

Welcome To The Machine was an early song and concept in which the group began to bemoan the highly successful situation they found themselves in. Some critics found this self-appraisal rather too fatuous for the group's own good, particularly when considering, for instance, the number of cars now owned by one member. The song lacked the breezy, happy-go-lucky attitude of The Byrds' *So You Want To Be A Rock'n'Roll Star*, being sung by Gilmour over a storm of synthesisers and keyboard effects generated by Wright. This sonic depiction of one man, his voice extended to its maximum extent, struggling to be heard over the machine in which he finds himself was however effective in its own bleak way; and at the time, fewer people than today had the cynicism required to grasp what forces lay behind the music industry. The music industry, after all, had only just stopped being the music business. So the metaphor of the machine was fitting – a device ensuring the smooth operation of industry; the product of an economic music revolution.

The snippets of machine sound worked perfectly with the near-dystopian vibe conjured up by the song, evoking something all-consuming, something monstrous, which ravaged every sonic avenue in its path. Yet for some critics, coming from a group who had only recently conquered the world, this evocation of despair and exploitation in the music world was a bit rich. It was akin to famous people complaining about their fame. Nevertheless, the song struck a chord for some. A decade or two had passed since the beginning of the Western domination of American technocratic capitalism, and British music was beginning to suffer from the same problems of scale and exploitation as bedevilled the American scene. *The Dark Side Of The Moon* had, in conspicuous style, conquered America. Now, a new, brash brand of capitalism was apparent to some in Britain. One of those was Roger Waters.

It is a moot point whether or not highly successful artists should whinge, diss, or otherwise talk down the situations they find themselves in after great success. In retrospect, and knowing everything about the history of Roger Waters since 1975, *Welcome To The Machine* could be seen as the beginning of his reputation for bitterness, in which he rails against the horrors of the world, takes sides, and generally acts in as provocative a manner as he likes. But in 1975, Waters knew nothing of this future. In 1967, he had been an innocent, allowed free rein to play in the fabulous playground of Abbey Road Studios. Yet that was only eight years previously. He had changed since '67, but not as much as he would by the time of his critically panned redux version of Pink Floyd's masterpiece. So it was not unreasonable that he observed the dark side of the industry in which he, by chance, without foresight and lacking any intention to dominate, found himself enmeshed. He lacked the experience to be bitter. He was just observing and commenting on something he at the time found relevant to his life. Only later would his accumulated strops, tirades, arguments and provocations make him look churlish.

The songs on side two of the LP continued in the same vein. *Have A Cigar* imagined a meeting between a grinning record company executive and an innocent musician, a kind of sequel to *Money,* and placed in the same LP position. It is a matter of great irony that because neither Waters nor Gilmour could summon up the gnarly insouciance required to sing the lyrics, they turned to a friend recording in a nearby studio, Roy Harper, who from his perspective, external to the group, and far less successful, had no difficulty at all in singing: *Oh, by the way, which one's Pink?*

Have A Cigar was the most traditional of the cuts on the album, but it was followed by one of the greatest of the acoustic, deeply felt songs that this group were capable of, which meant that in subsequent years it regularly appeared at or near the top of "best of Floyd" song lists. *Wish You Were Here* evoked both Waters himself and Syd Barrett. Written in happy moments of accord between Gilmour and Waters – moments destined to become rarer as the years passed – the song possessed lyrical weight and musical depth. It defined to perfection the ability of the members of the group to transform human experience into music and words, distilling what they felt in a way that for the group's millions of fans became their own experience. For everybody feels constrained by the world, distracted by the ephemera of capitalism, and most of us have the sense of failing to live in and enjoy the fleeting moments of life. Trapped in a fishbowl, lost, with no chance of redemption… Being English, the four men of Pink Floyd found themselves in the ideal position to convey this life experience.

This song was perfectly mixed into the album, beginning with a transistor radio scene in which Gilmour plays along with his AM self and ending with a slow, woozy fade into the latter half of the *Shine On You Crazy Diamond* composition. This concluding section was dominated by Wright's keyboards and synthesisers, showing just what a terrific musician he was, both as a composer and as a player. Gilmour played various guitars, including a lap steel, while Waters reprised his lyrics with aplomb. The final section was Wright solo, his synthesiser providing a marvellous, elegiac conclusion to the Barrett evocation; an ambient drift, a melancholy solo, then the slow fade into nothingness. It was a beautiful conclusion to the whole nine-part suite.

Syd Barrett, Pink Floyd and the music business were the core concepts of *Wish You Were Here,* but one event catapulted this album of regret and absence into something that, again by accident, acquired the weird lustre of music legend. Barrett, the lost genius, forever banished from his band, his mind sucked away by an LSD whirlpool, had not stopped writing and releasing music in the period following *Jugband Blues.* Indeed, David Gilmour was sometimes on hand to facilitate that process. But contact between the former songwriter and the globe-bestriding prog rock group were becoming less frequent.

On 5 June 1975, while the group were recording, Rick Wright walked into the mixing desk studio to observe a bald, fat man sitting a little way behind Roger Waters. Both men, over the next few minutes, told the other that they did not know who he was. Wright then watched as this unknown man got up and sat down again, and generally acted oddly. It was only some time later that he recognised the stranger. It was Syd Barrett himself.

I heard this story before I saw a printed copy of the single Polaroid photograph taken of Barrett on that extraordinary day. It was printed in Nick Mason's book *Inside Out.* For quite some time, I studied that photograph, unable to grasp that it was indeed Syd Barrett. It took me a while to see the resemblance in the eyes, and then, recalling the vibrant face of the psychedelic explorer from 1967 days, to understand that it really was Barrett. I then felt a sense of shock; that he had changed so much, that he had turned up in such extraordinary circumstances. Yet how much more devastating was it for the group, who knew him intimately? How much more shocking for Roger Waters, Barrett's childhood friend, to realise that even he had not recognised Barrett when his friend was sitting a few feet away? Later, Waters wept.

All four members of the group felt shocked, disturbed and upset by this incident. Barrett was not only heavy and fat, he had shaved off all his hair and his eyebrows. Looking at that remarkable Polaroid photograph even today generates a strange split. On the one hand, Barrett can just about be recognised by his eyes and some ghost present in his expression as he looks into the camera lens. On the other hand, it is easy to see a different man there. It could just be somebody a bit like him. But no. It really was him.

How I wish you were here…

By such strange coincidences are music legends made. The group, against all the odds, had crafted an LP fit to follow their 1973 epic. It was not itself epic, and its instrumentation was toned down from the intense sophistication of its predecessor. It did not address profound issues, rather satisfying itself with just one profound issue. Yet that focused intent made *Wish You Were Here* a truly great successor. It became a fan favourite, beloved and admired as much as *The Dark Side Of The Moon.* Eventual sales were a shade under half the former release, but sales are just one factor in an LP's life. The album acquired a different kind of shine. The 1973 release was multi-coloured and intense. The 1975 follow-up was muted and melancholy. But it had a kind of etiolated glamour that suited its tragic origin. It oozed a kind of class absent from its predecessor. Moreover, it was sincere. Nobody could doubt that in mining their own emotional hinterland, Pink Floyd had created the only kind of album that had a chance of following *The Dark Side Of The Moon* – on its *own* terms. In deciding to carry on from that impossible 1973, they had chanced upon a remarkable 1975. The album did not suffer in comparison to its predecessor. In the Syd Barrett appearance, it found its own mystical legend.

Even its cover became as recognisable as that iconic prism and spectrum from 1973. The Beatles, when releasing *The White Album,* had avoided any kind of image: a flat plane of white for the listener to project their fantasies onto. Pink Floyd took an image and turned it into a second icon. That was almost as remarkable an achievement as the album itself. In the music biz of the mid-1970s, getting burned meant being ripped off. The two men, one on fire, conveyed that notion of deceit, fraud and exploitation. The handshake symbolised empty rhetoric and empty promises – the music business norm. It was all Waters' discontent embodied in one memorable image. The LP itself, when it came out, was wrapped in anonymous black plastic, symbolising the absence of what lay inside. As a package, it worked as well as that for *The Dark Side Of The Moon.* The ill-tempered musings of music journalists had been countered in the most imaginative and heartfelt way possible. Once more, Pink Floyd had countered the malcontents of music journalism. They had done the impossible – followed a masterpiece. It could be argued that not even The Beatles had done that, if you count *Magical Mystery Tour* as a bona fide release. But, whatever the listener's perspective, *Wish You Were Here* was its own creation: unique, superb, emotive, challenging, profound.

After 1975, as thoughts of a new LP came into view, Roger Waters would increasingly become identified with the group, because of his lyrics and because of the album concepts he devised. But no album after *Wish You Were Here* would match its depth, reach and impact. There would be excellent albums, but no more iconic ones. Pink Floyd had in triumph ascended a double summit, but the landscape of British music was changing even as they toured, wrote and carried on bestriding the world. When *Wish You Were*

Here was released, a youth called John Lydon was strolling down London streets, the Pink Floyd on his defaced T-shirt prefixed with I HATE. When Syd Barrett visited the group in their studio, a new spirit of stripped-down, anti-prog music was being fermented in litter-strewn London streets. Across the Atlantic, new bands were pumping out a primal new music. Pink Floyd would not at first be affected by the rumours of a coming storm, but by the end of the decade, everything they knew about the music business was upended in a punk tsunami. Even they, the behemoth of prog who had reinvented themselves on numerous occasions, struggled to manage a complete change in the landscape.

Chapter 12

Animals

1976 was a strange year in rock music. There was a tension in the air, a tight lacuna in which many progressive rock groups took a breather. Something… nobody knew what exactly… something was *brewing* in Britain, some force from the underground, a cry from the street, a hint of thunder presaging a storm. But that storm as yet was concealed, unless you lived in central London, where a new music called punk rock was beginning to bubble up. Prog rock titans Yes, meanwhile, having lost yet another keyboard player, took time off to record a clutch of solo albums. Genesis managed to move on from the departure of Peter Gabriel and release *A Trick Of The Tail*, King Crimson were absent with leave after the exceptional *Red*, and Renaissance, having released a career highlight, *Scheherezade*, were also concealed somewhere in musical undergrowth. Other prog groups were beginning to lose the plot, notably ELP. For Pink Floyd, having sat back after a second iconic LP in two years, there was time to lounge around and play with their cars or guitars, as appropriate. That was not the whole story, however. With the EMI "unlimited time" contract out of action, the group decided to purchase property in Britannia Row, London, converting it into a new recording studio, in which they recorded the forthcoming album *Animals*.

This album was different from previous work in a number of ways. Early versions of the two tracks on the second side had been trialled and played the previous year, one of them called *Raving & Drooling*, and it was clear from the outset that Roger Waters was going to extend his influence within the group by not only finding the concept and writing most of the lyrics, but writing at least half of the music alone, with the side-long first track, *Dogs*, co-written with Gilmour. For the first time, Rick Wright did not get a writing credit. This was the first hint of tensions between the four Englishmen leading to trouble.

It is a curious fact that the theme of the album, worked up during 1975 and 1976, matched the themes of many of the early punk bands. Yet there was little or no connection, punk as yet being a tiny subculture in a minuscule part of London. Rather, punk youth and Roger Waters both observed the parlous state of the nation: economic regression, strikes and tussles, political chaos, and a sense that, following the energy crisis a few years earlier, something bad was happening in Britain – in slow motion, perhaps, and via a series of events originating far outside the island's coast, but something bad nevertheless. Britain was in a poor way. People had been calling it the sick man of Europe for a while now. Punks flailed out and expressed their inchoate anger inside the Roxy Club, and up and down a few local streets. Roger Waters, also railing against it all, and fuelled by an angst which was beginning to show itself loud and clear, decided to make the theme of *Animals* the inhumanity and perils of capitalism, how it affected communities, but especially how it made individuals lose something of their humanity. He would do this through the use of animals as metaphors: dogs, pigs, sheep. Each of these – the faithful dog, pigs which might fly (but, obviously, did not) and follow-the-leader sheep – was a metaphor for an inhumanity perpetrated by the system upon individuals. Faithful dogs which could attack if need be would themselves be callously treated, pigs, Orwell-style, would take over the system for their own benefit, while the masses, symbolised by flocks of sheep, would fail to question what was going on… until the end, when, in a weird subversion, they might try revolution.

Between 1975 and 1977, a great deal of development occurred in the field of keyboard and synthesiser technology. *Wish You Were Here* had utilised Wright's keyboards to a thrilling extent, with the string synthesiser notable, but on *Animals,* a new sound world came into view. On side one, it would be marked by a passage in the track *Dogs* which was haunting in its evocation of isolation. This section, set above a spectral drum pattern, used a whistling, keening synth solo to evoke feelings of eerie melancholy, around it a mutating set of chords that hovered and flew around the listener, against it, somebody whistling for the dog, and the dog barking. The new breed of synthesiser offered musicians of Wright's talent an expanded palette from which to choose. The middle section of *Dogs* showed the group once again creating vivid evocations of dark feelings, using high technology but in an original manner, one that highlighted the feeling, not the technology.

The track was composed by Waters and Gilmour, but Waters' presence was strong. Though Gilmour's guitar parts and solos for this track acquired a new chunky solidity, they lost none of their grace. His sound was changing a little, moving from the blues-inflected early 1970s sound to one rougher, gruffer, which would be best stated on his 1978 solo album and on *The Wall*.

Pigs was also a rocker, with a cooler instrumental section in the middle, one which built from slight components into something weird and visceral, the "pig noises" somewhere between porcine and human, the guitar part transmuted with electronic effects. It was mesmeric in its awful intensity, at once evoking slaughterhouses and the domineering pig ethic, perhaps the most obvious *Animal Farm* link on this album. Waters wrote the tune, and it served its purpose, though the listener could not help noticing the comparative lack of supple melody such as graced *Echoes* or *Us & Them*; something that was also true of the following cut, *Sheep*. The bass playing on *Pigs* however, was raised from Waters' usual stolid proficiency with dynamic runs and fills, adding propulsive power to the music. But Gilmour played the instrument, as he did on the following track.

Sheep was striking for the way Waters' vocal was transformed into a wailing, oscillating synthesiser note, as if his voice had been taken from its biological origin and cast into a brutal new technological mode. Stunning in its effect, those line-ending synthesiser parts would catch the listener's attention as the effect of the lyrics seeped into their mind, a union of music and word quite breathtaking. As the section closed, there was a cry and a peal of laughter too, emphasising the grotesque images conjured up by Waters' demolition of the capitalist mindset.

One of the significant features of the music on *Animals* was a kind of electronic voice which appeared on *Pigs* and *Sheep*. The machine making this was called a vocoder.

The principle of the vocoder had been around for a few decades by 1976. As early as the late 1950s, Siemens Studio For Electronic Music had built the Siemens Synthesiser, an early form of the device. The idea of the vocoder was a bit like radio, in which a carrier signal was modulated by a voice; in the vocoder's case, the carrier signal was provided by a synthesiser and the voice by a microphone. In 1968, Robert Moog created an early transistorised version at the music studios of Buffalo University in America. In 1970, Moog and Wendy Carlos designed an updated instrument using ten frequency bands, for which the resulting electronic voice was intelligible. The Moog was again the source of the sound to be modulated by the microphone output. As the 1970s continued, various bands used this novel sound, including ELP on *Brain Salad Surgery*. In West Germany, meanwhile, Kraftwerk were building their own custom vocoder and preparing to record the groundbreaking *Autobahn*, on which the device would be used.

For Pink Floyd, there was a sideways connection. Their gifted recording engineer for *The Dark Side Of The Moon*, Alan Parsons, had instituted his own group: The Alan Parsons Project. For his debut LP, the prog classic *Tales Of Mystery & Imagination*, inspired by the work of Edgar Allen Poe, the track *The Raven* used a modern example of the vocoder, whose voice output was high fidelity. Two years later, a vocoder would be used for *Animals*.

It was on *Sheep* that the clearest use was made. Roger Waters' mutated version of *The Lord's Prayer* was intoned by the voice of the vocoder, giving it a futuristic, unearthly timbre. It sounded as though some warning from a dystopian future had been received by the group, spoken by a robot. Yet on *Dogs*, the group's use of the vocoder transformed the sound of a dog barking into something eerie and chilling. For this section delivered from the perspective of the cast out hound, synthesised barking evoked the isolation and loneliness of the dog in a way quite unlike a normal recording. It was a triumphantly creative use of the vocoder with a nonhuman voice.

Another related technology was the talk box used by David Gilmour in the guitar solo for *Pigs*. Best known via the recordings of Peter Frampton, the mouth tube manipulated by the musician turned their amplified guitar into something similar to the vocoder, again giving the sound a futuristic timbre. In this case, the mouth itself changed the qualities of the guitar sound, which, acquiring speech-like components, sounded half guitar and half voice. All these vocoder and voice-style manipulations were glimpses of the future, both in music technology and of the world view conveyed by the album's concept. Both the vocoder and the talk box were masterful strokes of creativity.

The artwork for the album expanded on the style to which the group had recently become accustomed. As with the photographing of the two men, one alight, for *Wish You Were Here*, what was proposed was the staging and photographing of an event. This event would be set at and above Battersea Power Station, and was a depiction of the phrase "pigs might fly," referring to something that is never going to happen, but also to the pair of relatively uncynical songs bookending the LP. For nobody ever sees a pig on the wing.

Battersea Power Station on 2 December 1976 was the venue for that impossible sight. A huge pig balloon was fabricated, then allowed to float across the power station, with a marksman nearby in case the balloon broke away. As it happened, this did occur on the following day, when no rifle had been arranged to bring it down. Thus freed, the flying pig floated away, causing chaos at Heathrow. In the end, the album cover was composited from a photograph of the power station and an image of the pig balloon.

The cover solidified the reputation of Pink Floyd for striking album covers. *Meddle* and *The Dark Side Of The Moon* had both been somewhat accidental images, albeit created with intent; certainly, the latter, chosen the instant the group saw it, was a bit of a lucky break. Yet the image of the handshake between two men, one on fire, had been staged and photographed with great care. The covers for *Wish You Were Here* and *Animals* were elaborate theatrical fancies, indicative of the level of fame and influence the group had acquired since breaking through in 1973. Though they had become a vast enterprise, globally renowned and rich beyond the dreams of mortals, they remained in essence a quartet whose hearts lay in art as well as in music. Although the cultish, arty group had been abandoned at the gates of the moon's dark side, that arty spirit remained. The covers for the two albums emphasised the group's urge to create a striking image, one not created with an airbrush, but staged, enacted and photographed.

That was the Pink Floyd way. It was bold, innovative and wry.

Pigs On The Wing bookended the LP, relatively optimistic for Waters at this stage of his writing, with a warm acoustic feel that recalled the title track of the previous album. Yet this opener was a short song, providing mere glimpses of human warmth, which soon enough moved on to the terrors of *Dogs*. This track, written by Gilmour and Waters and sung by Gilmour, superbly conveyed the standard archetype of commercial capitalism, that dog-eat-dog world, where nobody feels true connection and everybody is taught to hide their feelings, and to show false feelings in preparation for making the kill. Everyone in this worldview was a killer, trained to perform on command by faceless, distant leaders. Dogs received a pat on the back if they were lucky. The training was tough, but everybody had a chance to perform with panache. Yet the corollary of this hierarchical system was that once the killer instinct had failed, had been tempered by age or by reflection, the master's dog was superfluous, and could be got rid of without compunction. Many such dogs had a large stone tied to them before they were flung into the nearest lake.

The song then turned to the subjective musing of that faithful hound cast aside. He was lost, confused, old and overweight in a late-life maze of callous carelessness. He was bitter, ill, alone. This, in Waters' vision, was the inevitable end of the capitalist functionary's life, exploited by the system, ill-used, trained for one purpose alone, then discarded when he just cannot carry on. It was a vision of a world of emotionally distant relationships entirely unlike that hinted at by the soft, soothing opening cut. Dogs ate other dogs. Capitalism favoured the winner only. Nobody remembered who came second. For Waters, observing exactly that injustice in the British voting system (there had already been three general elections in half a decade), the inhumanity of the system was plain. It was a masculine, vicious, callous competition of winners who took all. It emphasised the importance of the individual – the winner, the MP, the rich man, the CEO, the leader, the upper-class gentleman, the captain, the bishop, the judge. There was no place for community in this world view, no mechanism for individuals to join one another in theatres of human warmth. Relationships were mediated by telephone, and everyone at home was a stranger to each other. Big dogs ruled the country, and they used smaller dogs to do their dirty work.

This was a brutal view. Commentators debated its accuracy and relevance following the album's release, but there was no doubting Waters' unerring skill in picking up on one of the main consequences of capitalism, its utter lack of regard for those not at the top of the economic tree.

Pigs (Three Different Ones) was a reflection on those who had reached their own particular summit. Waters here showed even less mercy on his subjects. The pigs included that straight-laced guardian of the nation's morals, Mary

Whitehouse, mentioned by name and described as a "house proud town mouse." Meanwhile, the porcine CEOs of the country were depicted as fat and greasy-lipped, having consumed so much of the nation's produce. It was a vivid demolition of the captains of industry and other self-appointed or Tory-appointed masters of the British economic landscape, seen by Waters as selfish to a grotesque degree. The metaphor of the pig was well-earned.

Capitalism had been called "enlightened self-interest" by most of its critics, and even by a few of its apologists, but what was often missed at the time was how capitalism emphasised and amplified the Western view of the individual being more important than the group. In the East, for instance, in China and Japan, the opposite was true, leading in the case of China to a different kind of political obscenity – mass oppression. Communism could never have worked in the West because it was at heart a philosophy lumping a vast number of people into a tiny number of social identities. In China, there was no difficulty with that. But, in London, Roger Waters saw how the self-interest part of "enlightened self-interest" was the key to the nature of capitalism and the way the pigs always rose to the top. Doubtless, he took something from George Orwell's masterful *Animal Farm* in that. Self-interest had nothing to do with enlightenment.

Sheep, meanwhile, was an evocation of the blind, bleating masses. Capitalism and the British class system in general relied for much of their efficacy on the misleading of the masses, blinding them with hypnotic advertising, lying about political and economic realities, and pretending that the natural order of things in Britain was based on unchanging historical truth. This, the sheep accepted without complaint, or even any thought. They were happy in their muddy pastoral idyll, eating grass, pretending there were no dogs about and that no pigs were enjoying the good life at the top of the tree.

But in Waters' evocation of British capitalism, there was a shock on the way. After a significantly changed version of *The Lord's Prayer* in which the shock-artists are themselves shocked, the sheep rise up and fall upon their lords and masters with screams of vengeance. For there is news in the land! The dogs are dead. Yet even this good news has a cynical consequence to it. There will be new masters. If the sheep wish to reach old age, what they have to do is get out of the way. In Waters' view, the exploited would always be unaware of the chains in which they lived, chains owned in the main by pigs and big dogs. It was that lack of awareness of their condition that struck Waters most deeply. To escape their cell, a prisoner first has to be aware that they are imprisoned. As Marx had it: you have nothing to lose but your chains. For Waters, those chains were capitalist illusions given deep roots by the unjust, top-heavy British ruling class, for whom sleight of hand was a crucial art. But people need something to believe in. Illusions would have to do. Waters was railing against that lack of effort as much as he was railing against the system itself.

Ironically, in the year *Animals* was released, the first, most shocking, most efficacious and longest-lasting consequence of British conservatism and lack of social insight was unleashed. Punk rock did for young people and in the most furious manner possible what Waters was trying to do in his own social circle. Punk was a cry of fury in circumstances of intense frustration. At last, John Lydon and so many others of his ilk saw the chains that had been confining them, and they were not happy about living in prison cells. Yet it was not only Roger Waters in the group who grasped the significance of the punk explosion. Nick Mason also realised what was going on, and soon enough was in charge of producing *Music For Pleasure*, the latterly adored but at the time dismissed, even mocked, second album by punk pioneers The Damned.

Punk changed everything, although not at once and with varying consequences. Pink Floyd would be touched by punk as, with 1977 running out, they pondered their next move. Yet it turned out that, in fact, it was mostly Roger Waters considering Pink Floyd's next move.

For all the musical ambition and widescreen songwriting of *Animals* – one of the very best albums in their canon – it cannot match the iconic status of *The Dark Side Of The Moon* and *Wish You Were Here*. Those two albums enjoy a unique position, not only amongst fans but worldwide, and even outside the field of music. Yet *Animals* cannot quite compete. Why is this?

The former two albums both employ forms of social criticism which have deep roots in Roger Waters' personal concerns. Even as far back as *Take Up Thy Stethoscope And Walk*, he made this stance plain through his lyrics. Both of those iconic albums, unlike *Animals*, strike the listener from an internal perspective. *The Dark Side Of The Moon* especially is a dramatisation of the verities of the human condition, rendered in a universal style yet achingly personal too. That mode was repeated with even more pathos for *Wish You Were Here,* in which a universal experience, that of loss and grief, was dramatised. In the former case, the human experiences, evoked for the listener via their stereophonic headphones as if from their own perspective, were death, life, madness, money and war. Every listener was given the opportunity to immerse themselves in this forty-minute cinematic journey, to feel that *they* were being spoken to, like some authors do to their readers through their choice of theme and narrative rendering. With *Wish You Were Here,* the universal experience of losing somebody close was evoked. This was Syd Barrett, of course, whose friendship with Waters preceded Pink Floyd by many years. Yet we have all experienced the tragedy of loss. We all know the pain. Rendered by the group as if from a personal perspective, that second album duly acquired its iconic status.

Animals had no less of a concept than those of the two albums which preceded it, yet it was rendered from an external perspective. The bitter critique of the lyrics are addressed as if to capitalism itself, with the listener looking on a little like a voyeur watching a horror film through their fingers. Very little by way of an internal human perspective is evoked, although *Dogs* comes closest to that. This change in perspective gave the album more of a didactic quality, making it less personal, though in terms of its subject matter it was just as important. Yet the overall impact was in the main from the outside of human experience: exploitation illustrated, sheepish acceptance exposed, and the dog-eat-dog world that capitalism fosters made plain, as if in some ghoulish Francis Bacon painting.

When creating the concepts for the two iconic albums, Waters mined his *own* character; his own psychological depths. He did this too when writing their lyrics. All his own feelings about the lure of money and the rock star life, the human truths of life and death, the possibility of madness and the inevitability of grief and horror through war, and the tragedy of loss, came out in that period of exceptional creativity. And this is often the way with art that stands the test of time and is universally admired. The authors of those creations, be they iconic novels, films or LPs, mine their own truths. Whether they realise it or not, their own experiences, especially of suffering, become transformed into universal experiences conveyed by culture.

The author A.N. Wilson made this point in his brilliant book *The Mystery Of Charles Dickens*. In it, he posited the idea that, had Dickens not suffered during his childhood, or had he enjoyed access to counselling or other forms of psychological support during his younger years, he probably would not have written novels with so profound a level of human insight. It was the unconscious motivation of his unresolved psychological dilemmas that gave his insight – which he poured into each of those marvellous novels – such keen and memorable value. Had he resolved his childhood issues, he may never have written with such heart-rending insight.

Waters dipped his toes into his own personal well for the outstanding song *Echoes*, and he would do it twice again across whole LPs. But by 1976 he had plumbed his own depths. For whatever reason, his keen and insightful glance was thrown elsewhere.

To create *Animals*, Waters mined an external entity – the mode of social organisation known as capitalism. This was just as fruitful when it came to themes, structure and details, but it lacked the internal psychological depiction which made the former pair of albums iconic. It described a human reality – capitalism and all the damage that economic system wreaked – but said little about interior consequences. There was vivid depiction and marvellous images, but not much by way of *verity*. For that reason, the album can be regarded as brilliant but not iconic.

A couple of days before writing this section I googled: *Why is Roger Waters so angry?* This search threw up a number of interesting results.

There is no doubt in my mind that the reason Waters, especially, but also the other three members of the group, created two exceptional and revered LPs was that, most likely without realising it, they were created by mining their own psychological depths. That process is best done without comprehension; at least, if you want to make great art. Without such realisation, albums like *The Dark Side Of The Moon* and *Wish You Were Here* arrive. When you *do* realise what is going on with your own creativity, a level of comprehension appears, and with it a way of changing the focus of unconscious inspiration – a quality of *deliberation*, making it conscious and directed. Without knowing you are mining your own psychological depths, you get *The Dark Side Of The Moon*. When you do know, you reach *The Wall*.

Small, English, polite tensions had been bubbling up in the group for a while, as Waters took a more emphatic hold of the group. Wright had been sidelined in a strange, almost casual manner, receiving no writing credit for any of the music on *Animals*. Yet it turned out that he had written plenty of songs, and they were very good ones. As 1977 turned into 1978, he retired to Super Bear Studios in France to record the songs that would form his first solo album, *Wet Dream*. This delightful LP had most of the classic Wright touches: his laconic, yet vulnerable style of singing, in which his speaking voice was central, the reliance on keyboards, and plenty of classic Wright chord and key changes. Some of the tracks were instrumentals, some were sung. Although it was recorded at the beginning of the year in little more than one month, it was not released until autumn 1978. It was a mark of how Pink Floyd were viewed that it failed to chart and indeed appeared to have been made available under a media blackout. The impact was minimal. Perhaps that had as much to do with David Gilmour's solo LP release a few months earlier, but it also spoke of Wright being the "quiet one" of Pink Floyd, at least, outside the group's core fan base.

Four months earlier, in late spring, David Gilmour – who had gone to Super Bear Studios directly after Wright departed – released *David Gilmour*, an equally strong collection of his own songs. That album was more visible and did chart. It remains beloved amongst Floyd fans, is as marvellous a listening experience forty-five years later as it was then, and is notable amongst many other qualities for emphasising the hard-edged, chugging guitar sound that Gilmour was in the process of developing.

Gilmour at the time remarked that being in a rock group can be a somewhat claustrophobic existence, and stepping out for a while to deliver his own songs was a consequence of that. Although this remark was accepted as not unreasonable at the time, it was an early indication that the balance of influence within the group was not equitable, and that there would be consequences. How much more was that imbalance felt by Wright, who in just a couple of years would be unceremoniously sacked in the second of the catastrophes to affect this most taciturn of rock groups. Nick Mason was also considering solo work, but the results of that thought process would not appear until 1981.

That the guitarist and keyboardist of the group released excellent solo albums of their own songs in 1978 could have been regarded as indicative of the creative power of those two musicians. To an extent, that was true. But critics had also noticed the increasingly prominent role played by Waters. They loved his concepts and admired his lyrics, but the drift in influence and power was in plain view. The writing was on the wall.

Chapter 13

The Wall

When I was nineteen and a physics student at university in leafy Surrey, I spotted a notice stuck to a wall amidst a blizzard of other notices. It advertised two tickets for sale for one of the upcoming Pink Floyd concerts at Earls Court in London. This was June 1981, and I was about to finish my first year at university. I'd seen Tangerine Dream the year before, and was getting used to the idea of going into central London on the train to attend concerts. I had bought *The Wall* LP, and was a fan. I'd listened to Tommy Vance interviewing Roger Waters on the radio, and was impressed. The bit where Vance described the lyrics to *One Of My Turns* as rather depressing stuck in my mind; and Waters' response – "I love it!"

Being naïve, shy and awkward, I didn't grasp the significance of the girl selling the tickets withdrawing the second one after I bought the first. She decided she was going to go after all, and sit next to me, at the rear and the right of the auditorium. We met again as I sat beside her that evening. My memory of her and any conversation fails me now, forty-five years later, but one thing I do remember about us (with regret) is that somehow we got separated in the mass exodus for buses and trains. I don't recall any contact afterwards in those last few days of term.

My memory of the gig, however, is vivid. The Stuka aeroplane on its high wire… the slow building of the wall in huge white bricks as the concert progressed… the floating schoolmaster, mother and wife, and another floating pig… David Gilmour's guitar solo for *Comfortably Numb* on his high podium… Gerald Scarfe's gobsmacking animations, projected throughout the show… the little hole inside the wall representing Pink's hotel room… and the demolition of the wall for the final song, then the group emerging to receive their applause. An unforgettable evening! Outside, shuffling from merch vendor to merch vendor, I bought a white sweatshirt as a memento; didn't wear it much, as it was a pretty poor fit.

I was a confirmed fan of the group by then, with most of their LPs, and even a few bootlegs on tape, recorded from Uni friends who owned these exotic vinyl objects. I enjoyed the new album a lot, played it, and had favourite songs. I grasped something of its background, but lacked the insight and education to place it in its appropriate context. Yet something odd happened through the years that followed. Although I played earlier albums regularly, *The Wall* dropped off my play list, and, in the end, never returned. At the time, with so much amazing music to enjoy, I didn't ponder why that might be. Now, however, I have the insight and the time to wonder why this album is no longer a favourite and is never played. For I didn't replace my original LP with a CD version, nor will I.

Many music fans place themselves on one side or the other of *The Wall*: like/dislike. I've done the same thing.

For Roger Waters, undertaking the *In The Flesh* world tour of 1977, things were getting difficult. In the Tommy Vance interview, Waters related an incident in which some of the group's fans were enjoying the music in a noisy, exhibitionist way, which conveyed to Waters the fact that they were not listening to the music at all. It was just a night out for them, a chance to freak out and lose themselves in a rock music spectacle. Any old band would have sufficed. Suddenly angered, Waters leaned over and spat on one of the men.

This incident shocked him. He spoke about it to friends that same night. While Gilmour and Wright were away in France recording their solo albums and Mason was producing an LP by Gong's beanie-wearing guitar wizard Steve Hillage, Waters worked up concepts for two LPs, one of them relating to the alienation he felt as part of the music industry. This, in time, would become *The Wall*.

But this was an album quite different from *Animals*. It was, in effect, a rock opera. Waters, as he had since 1972, created a concept for an entire work, which this time would be extended to a double LP. And this was a big concept, one of two he had presented to the group after the success of *Animals*. *The Wall*, however, contained more autobiographical elements than anything Waters had previously created. It was to be the story of a jaded, drug-addled rock star called Pink. But Pink was not a creature of imagination and nothing else. Pink emerged from Waters' experience during the In The

Flesh Tour, where he had spat on a fan freaking out. Pink also exhibited elements of Syd Barrett, as the film made afterwards would show – shaved head and shaved eyebrows.

The album opened with a bombastic rock cut called *In The Flesh?* whose title echoed the name of the tour during which the spitting incident occurred. There was a live feel to the recording, hinting at a huge, globally successful rock band playing some international tour date to a stadium audience. As the song progressed, Waters (the main vocalist for this album) started to break down the barrier between himself and the imaginary live date – known to actors as the fourth wall – by issuing a stream of commands to the stage technicians: *Lights! Roll the sound effects! Action!* As an aeroplane began a terrifying dive-bomb manoeuvre, the song came to its climax, then cut in a fraction of a second to the sound of a baby crying. This referred to a real birth, but also to a more conceptual birth, that of one man damaged by the hellish circumstances of war.

The Thin Ice, at first sung by Gilmour, was a song about the perils of growing up. There was a soft, lullaby feel to the piece, evoking the coddled ease of childhood. But when Waters took up the song lyrics, the atmosphere became more ominous, even tortured. Waters had, on previous albums, sung little more or less than Gilmour, using his slightly nasal voice to good effect. On this album, however, he developed a more tortured style of singing that involved harder and deeper breathing as well as a constriction of the throat. When the full group came in after his vocal, the sound returned to that bombastic vibe announced by the opening track. It presaged horrors to come…

There followed one of the album's most recognisable sounds and riffs. Gilmour, for this LP, developed a delayed sound that gave motion and panoramic width to his playing. *Another Brick In The Wall (Part 1)* used this to superb effect, as Waters sang of the loss of a father, with memories the only thing remaining. Yet this was not just Pink's father lost in World War II. Waters himself had lost his father, a catastrophic family event that informed a lot of the album and much of the solo work which followed. The song had a great and memorable melody, leading at its conclusion to a range of vocal effects – various voices, whistles, and the noise of kids at school. Gilmour's mesmeric guitar underpinned all this. These sound effects of childhood and life at school introduced the next song, *The Happiest Days of Our Lives,* a title intended to use as much sarcasm as possible. Following the famous Pink Floyd helicopter sound, the listener was introduced to the sadistic teachers of Pink's "happy school days" – which they clearly were not. There was not much of a tune to this song, but the vocal style – part snarled, part muttered – made clear the nightmare of school life for Pink. Half-screeched orders to children delivering impossible targets and semi-insane requirements – you can't have your pudding if you haven't finished your meat – were awful in their intensity. For all listeners whose school days were miserable and filled with torment, this was a recapitulation visceral in its intensity.

Yet the song concluded with a remarkable turnaround. In the words of what became a most unexpected hit song, *Another Brick In The Wall (Part 2): We don't need no education...* And thus the children turned everything around. The song was a fight back, addressed to the teachers, admonishing them, telling every cane-wielding bully to leave them alone. Gilmour sang this song, and provided one of the most celebrated guitar solos in rock history, whose sublime slides and bends turned that recording into the sonic equivalent of a fluid, mutable and flexible in his masterful hands. With the addition of a children's choir and a memorable video, it was a worldwide smash hit, reaching the top of the charts in Britain, America and many other countries. This boosted sales of the album, which at the time was receiving mixed reviews.

The last song on the first side of the LP was more reflective, but, in the context of the album as a whole, much more ominous. *Mother* was a song about Pink back at home, bruised and battered by his experiences of loss, of sadistic school masters, and a life of grim heartbreak. Waters was the voice of this young person at home, asking sometimes whimsical, sometimes profound questions of his mother, with Gilmour singing the mother's replies. Yet those replies were smothering. They wrapped Pink in a soft barrier, a wall that Waters had hinted at when he demanded *Lights! Action!* and which, it transpired, were the beginning of the building of the LP's wall, made from bricks of pain and despair. This song transformed the gruelling experiences of wartime loss, of senseless thuggery at school and of a family life that insulated Pink from the outside world into the harsh realities of the rest of the album. In these brutal childhood experiences was sown the character of Pink himself. This beaten Pink lacked confidence, lacked vision, felt uncertain. He was small and nearly mute, his voice beaten out of him by cane and fist. And yet… his mother might let him sing.

The LP so far was conceptually sound, executed to a high standard, psychologically acute and dramatically brilliant, yet it did lack something. That something was the keyboards of Rick Wright.

The second side of the album dealt with Pink's adolescent years and his semi-reluctant slide into the world of rock music. *Goodbye Blue Sky* was a song that ached with nostalgia for a ruined childhood. It evoked the un-lived golden days, the unremembered happiness of a child's life, those endless summer days which, for Pink, are never experienced. These painful memories made for a melancholy song.

Empty Spaces had an almost industrial feel to it, with churning, chugging machine sounds making a dramatic rhythm track that suggested mental pain, fear, self-torture. Waters then sang, bringing the psychological chaos to life. This was a song that literally built the wall in circumstances of silence, lack of communication, barriers and the dark, desolate spaces of the title – the spaces between people. The oppressive sonic vibe was an analogy of mental darkness, of the building of a psychological wall for protection, from pain, from chaos, from abuse and wartime madness impossible to control, let alone manage. It was a song of psychological survival, of living in a mode that forbade anything other than the basics.

The song then burst into *Young Lust,* in which, having been allowed to sing by his mother, Pink got into the rock 'n' roll life – groupies and all. It was a hedonistic, freewheeling song delivered to perfection by Gilmour's vocal and guitar. The rock solo was classic Gilmour, encapsulating the "new boy in town" looking for a good time. This song however, ended with one of the many consequences of Pink's mental state – his inability to communicate. A phone call (recorded without the knowledge of the American operator, whose acting was therefore perfect) is picked up, but no communication ensues. It was another metaphor for the abyss being created between Pink and the people around him.

There followed two of the crucial tracks on the album, and two of the best. Moreover, these were the only tracks that sounded as though Rick Wright had serious input, via his shimmering, glossy keyboards. Wright, however, his relationship with Waters deteriorating, was forced to resign from the group during recording, leading to most of the keyboards on this album, while proficient, evoking little more than standard rock sounds. There was no Wright magic. *Don't Leave Me Now* and *One Of My Turns* were black, despairing depictions of the woozy turmoil of Pink's mental distress, filled with the sounds of breathing and Waters' increasingly cracked and tortured vocal style. As an evocation of incipient madness, they were superb, if harrowing. The television blanketed all possibility of communication between Pink and the groupie he has brought back from a gig, she speaking, he ignoring. Then: Hello? Are you feeling okay?

In the lengthy interview with BBC Radio 1 DJ Tommy Vance when the LP was released, Waters spoke about this track, with Pink bemoaning his horrible life. Vance put it to him that this track, with its lyric, "Dry as a funeral drum," was a bit depressing. Waters just laughed and replied that he loved it.

It is a moot point whether or not Waters went too far with this rock opera. The sense of madness and regret evoked by these two songs is brilliantly done, yet it is not just Pink feeling isolated and depressed: it is Waters too. So, although there is deep psychological acuity in this concept of a wall, of mental barriers founded in chaos, pain and confusion, there is also a balancing factor, which is the self-serving squalor of the average arrogant rock star. Waters places himself there, and that, perhaps, is fair enough. He had the experience. He felt a wall. He spat. But it did not help that he kept on doing it, ensuring there were more occasions for listeners to feel sorry for him.

At the end of this pair of tracks, a television is smashed. At the end of the first, Pink smashes a window and dares the groupie to encourage him to fly – all brilliantly dramatised.

Another Brick In The Wall (Part 3) was short and brutal. Suddenly, the self-loathing Pink was the strong Pink. The sad, soft Pink was the steel-reinforced Pink. The pink Pink was the hairless, hard Pink. In moments, he had turned from being melancholy to pushing his anger and pain deep inside. He had become tough, macho, callous, brutal. He was an authoritarian now. He was nearly a fascist. *Goodbye Cruel World* was a short lament sung by Waters, a song about the final schism between an individual and his world. The final "goodbye" of the song is heard without reverb, as if spoken one inch from the listener's ear. *Goodbye.* Side three of the LP began with

Hey You, sung by Gilmour, a song about trying to connect with an audience. Pink in this song needed to break through, to find people in the barren, desolate world outside himself. Acutely aware of the wall through seeing his fans but not feeling them, he started to feel the worms of decay taking their inevitable toll. But here Pink needed to cling on to hope. He was apart, a brute, callous and strong in authority, yet there was a tiny voice inside still hoping for humanity.

Is There Anybody Out There? saw the return of the television, that pointless, omnipresent voice speaking 24/7 while saying nothing at all. An ominous synthesiser underpinned Waters' hushed vocal: Is there anybody out there? The briefest hint of the seagull sound and a ping! from *Echoes* once again signified Pink's need for empathy above all else – for connection, for the experience of somebody else understanding. This dramatic interval led into a solo acoustic guitar piece, evoking the quiet desperation that is the English way…*Nobody Home* wrung the maximum amount of pathos from Pink bemoaning his lack of a girlfriend and his inability to fly. It was schlocky and clumsy, and led into a pair of songs that emphasised the importance of wartime experiences to young Pink. *Vera* asked if anybody could remember Vera Lynn, while *Bring The Boys Back Home* began with boots marching, before heading off into a song too full of pride for its own good. The brass section and choir only served to emphasise points that were already too obvious. It was a sudden lack of grace and surety that led to Waters' most tortured vocal…a screech too far this time. Then sound effects recapitulated the album so far; a knock on the door. Pink, it's time for your concert!

Yet Pink is not quite ready. In *Comfortably Numb,* one of this group's most celebrated songs, he recalls the experience of being bitten and given a numbing medicine – an autobiographical incident that at once evokes the naivete of childhood and the need for comfort of any sort, even that provided by drugs. In this song, Waters is again trying to connect with his authentic, inner self, his real, human self, now locked away by a stark and towering wall. Gilmour here provides the perspective of Pink, adding one of his finest guitar solos. I remember seeing and hearing this solo at the live version I attended in 1982, with Gilmour isolated by his solitary position and the sharp-focus spotlight. Unforgettable!

The final side of the LP comprised the gig that Pink must perform. *The Show Must Go On* featured choral vocals and Gilmour singing, in a call-and-respond style. This was real rock opera stuff, albeit with hints of 10cc and the Alan Parsons Project. Pink here was preparing for the concert, but his authoritarian tendencies were coming to the fore. Is he okay – all there? Is he sane, stable? Will he remember the song? *In The Flesh* kicked off the gig, recapitulating the opening track, but here the ghastly fascist hints of earlier were given free reign, as Pink, strong through isolation, hard through protecting himself against pain, becomes a terrifying figure of intolerance. Are there any queers in the audience? Any Jews? And other minorities… In a shotgun stanza, Pink decides he would have all of them killed, including those smoking joints, and even just with adolescent spots. It was a shocking anti-fan rant, a dehumanising act of cold fury.

Run Like Hell dramatised what followed. The concert became a fascist outburst, gang violence, taunts and shrieking tyres: a rampage, a Kristallnacht. Against Gilmour's delayed, looping guitar this fascist rally took place, the drums banging out their martial rhythm. Waters, singing as Pink, was the hunter, the ultra-right-wing figurehead. It truly was a nightmare.

Waiting For The Worms opened with a faux-German introduction before heading off into *Goodbye Cruel World* territory, in which Pink was safe inside his bunker, within the encircling wall. But the worms here were a metaphor for decay. Pink's fascism could not last. His perfect isolation could not save him. The worms of decay were everywhere, respecting no man, sensing no wall. Yet a megaphone voice still shouted out the fascist mantra, weeding out the weaklings, referring to a final solution, to Kristallnacht, to showers and ovens.

The message was clear. You just need to follow. That is all there is to it. You just need to send the undesirables home. This was akin to National Front hatred. Brutal, callous, authoritarian. And as the crowd shouted, "Hammer! Hammer! Hammer!" Pink was faced with the consequences of his deeds. He saw all the horror and brutality.

Stop!

In *Stop*, Pink deflated. He sank back. The steel-reinforced facade was not strong enough. Now he was in a cell. Had he been guilty all this time…?

The album now concluded. With Pink aghast at what he had become, he put himself on trial in a piece that managed neither to fit the preceding music nor give a satisfying answer to the dilemma of Pink and all those like him. *The Trial* was a mock opera, sung by Waters in the most shaky of assumed accents and with the least musical of accompaniments. As a key opened the cell door, Pink put himself on trial, a process during which the judge got to see the horrors, terrors and brutality of his childhood. The prosecution explained that Pink was guilty of showing feelings – no fascist should ever do that. Feelings of an almost human nature, which would not do. That was the crime. But the judge saw it differently. Taking into account the smothering mother, the wartime trauma, the sadistic teachers and chaotic adolescence, he gave his verdict, that the wall must be torn down. Pink, said the judge, had revealed his deepest fear. This gave him one chance of redemption. There was a door in the wall all that time. Pink, therefore, had to be exposed.

Outside The Wall found Pink dazzled by his first experience of the outside world since building the wall. The music is suitably quiet and reflective. For, all this time, it has just been some mad bugger's wall…

Some say *The Wall* is a work of genius. Some say it is not. I bought the LP when it came out, I watched the single and its video climb to the top of the charts, and I got to love the music. Through the 1980s I would listen to the album, yet by the end of the decade I had stopped. Somehow, I just didn't find it as attractive as the earlier albums, and, indeed, as *A Momentary Lapse Of Reason* when that appeared. Why was this? Why, when I came to prepare for this chapter, had well over twenty years passed since my last listen to *The Wall?* Why was I dreading returning to it?

The two iconic 1970s albums were dramatisations of universal human themes, *interior* themes, which any and all human beings could grasp, understand and enjoy. They were thrilling in their intensity and relevance. *Animals* was superb, but it was a depiction of an exterior reality: Capitalism. In that, its theme, important without doubt, was not so universal. Its exterior quality made it specific, not fundamental. *The Wall* returned the listener to an interior landscape, that of Pink, but Pink was partially modelled on Roger Waters, not on a universal human being. It was therefore highly specific. That specific landscape, semi-autobiographical, meant that, for me at least, once I had grasped and comprehended the messages of the album, I was done.

The music of *The Wall* is alright. I am damning it with faint praise, of course. Good though that music is, it is neither as superb as that of *Animals*, nor as exceptional as that of *Wish You Were Here* and *The Dark Side Of The Moon*. Indeed, what really struck me on my most recent listen prior to the writing of this chapter was the enormous hole left by the absence of Rick Wright. In some ways, Waters managed here to squeeze a lot of the Floyd out of Pink Floyd, leaving only Pink; and Pink was pretty much himself. This album sounds stark. In places, it even sounds trite. Stripped down, with Gilmour on fine form but not enough of Wright and his beautiful keyboards, the group making *The Wall* is almost not Pink Floyd. With those standard organs and minimal keyboards, it could be any old band fronted by Waters, with Gilmour in attendance. The emphasis on lyrics, story and concept can conceal the fact that the music here, while alright, is not particularly memorable, except for a few classic moments. But if only *Comfortably Numb* and that No. 1 single are remembered and mentioned now, what is left? All those tracks that people forget the titles of. The rest of the LP.

This, I think, explains why I don't want to listen to *The Wall* as often as I do *Animals* or *Wish You Were Here*. The concept and lyrics of *The Wall* are superb, but the music that accompanies them is only good. Once the story has been grasped and the setting enjoyed, there is little to go back for; *Comfortably Numb* and *Another Brick In The Wall*, but little else. *Animals*, on the other hand, with its concept and lyrics just as good, has the music required to support it and create a truly marvellous album, a Floydian fusion of concept, words and music, one that rewards time after time. *The Wall does* reward, but once that is over there is little left.

I vividly remember the moment at the end of the 1981 Earls Court concert when the group walked on stage in front of the demolished wall and waved farewell to us. Suddenly – so suddenly it took my breath away – I realised that there, a hundred yards away, was the *real* Pink Floyd, four human beings that until then I had only known from their music, reviews in the music papers, and the occasional radio or television appearance. These four human beings on stage *were* Pink Floyd. In that moment the conceptual gap between me and them dissolved. A moment of connection, albeit only in my own mind, was created, between myself and that musical entity.

If Roger Waters wanted to heal the division between himself and the audience, that was probably all he had to do. Come out and wave. And he *did* have to do it. He had to do something following his inspirational gob.

The Wall is a concept of psychological authenticity and great depth. It is a work showing how trauma makes hard-edged monsters of men in particular, the authoritarians of this world, the dictators, the brutes, the fascists. It shows how, by ignoring human connection, those soft, warm feelings that women are allowed to acknowledge but men are not, people become disconnected, hard, self-loathing and inauthentic. Life is squeezed out of them by politics and by conservatism, which, in the hands of those without scruples, becomes bog-standard right-wing tradition. The transformation of Pink from traumatised youth to fascist leader is psychologically true. It has happened throughout history. It is happening now, even in liberal Western countries. We need the message of *The Wall* now more than ever. And that is a horrible irony.

Roger Waters has been vocal for decades on political matters, to the satisfaction of some and the fury of others. His comments in support of Palestinians and the illegal occupation of Palestinian land are seen by some as antisemitism. Yet criticising the brutal foreign policy of Israel is not by any means the same as being antisemitic, for the same reason that criticising the blood-stained colonial past of Britain is not anti-British. These comments merely acknowledge reality.

What is far more perplexing and problematic is Waters' comments on Vladimir Putin, whom, if reporting is to be believed, Waters feels has been mischaracterised as a dictator. Some have gone so far as to say that Waters supports Putin in that man's war on Ukraine. Some see Waters having some understanding, perhaps even empathy with Putin.

Most of us in the West see Putin as a dictator whose desire is to keep as tight a control of Russia for as long as possible. It is therefore baffling to us when we read of Waters' comments. He seems to have turned in his old age, rather like John Lydon making an advert for butter.

Yet, in the context of *The Wall,* that psychologically acute depiction of the creation of a dictator from a traumatised child, we can perhaps see something more explicable. Pink is not Roger Waters. But Pink does manifest some of Waters' traits. Waters' original concept was more autobiographical at the start, but producer Bob Ezrin refined and improved the concept until it became the album we know. Yet in Pink, attracted through self-imposed isolation to concepts of authoritarianism and brutal monoculture, we see all authoritarians. We see all dictators. We see all warmongers. Pink is not just isolated. He is doing what so many of us do – denying our pain, stopping our pain from being felt, transforming our pain into patterns of behaviour. Putin is not Pink, nor Waters, but in Putin's deeds, character and manner, we see the results of psychological trauma. Waters knows this.

Whether Waters is attracted to Putin as a dictator because of his own unresolved trauma, or whether he is repulsed but sees Putin with an insight that we, who did not suffer as Waters did, do not, is a question for those who know the man personally. Yet, in a book about Pink Floyd with a chapter on *The Wall*, we have to make these comparisons and ask these questions, even if such things must, alas, remain obscure. It is worth remembering however, that Pink is not just about Roger Waters; he is about Syd Barrett too. Waters and Barrett were childhood friends. In seeing Barrett lose his mind, Roger Waters experienced another traumatic loss that deeply marked his character and life.

Sensitive people do not interact with the world in the way that everybody else does. High sensitivity is a biologically ordained trait that we, the highly sensitive, have no control over. Such sensitive individuals often become musicians, or, if not, have a deep, rich and complex relationship with music. It is no stretch of the imagination to see such sensitivity in Waters and Gilmour, and perhaps in Wright too. But highly sensitive people facing trauma have to erect barriers far higher and more extensive than those of their friends and family. Such barriers must come into force and operate at a much lower level of tolerance. It is not so absurd to see in Roger Waters' metaphorical wall the towering barrier needed by a sensitive, perhaps highly sensitive man, who experienced more loss and trauma than his mind was able to manage; not just his father, but Syd too.

Many find Waters abrasive, misguided, misogynistic and bitter. We would do well to consider the man himself, his life and times, and wonder how such a circumstance came about. One of our clues is *The Wall*.

Chapter 14

The Final Cut

I remember listening to *The Final Cut* for the first time when it came out. It sounded wet. It sounded limp. It sounded defeated. In Roger Waters' tortured vocals, I heard something I had never noticed before. That was the sound of whinging.

The Wall was a brilliant concept. Rooted in personal experience, it spoke to its listeners, many of whom had been forced to endure the same suffering as Waters. It teased out insightful and well-dramatised aspects of the authoritarian tendencies of the twentieth century and presented them with flair. Some thought, like so many double LPs of the 1970s, that it would have been a better three-sided LP, but that would probably have been commercial suicide. Only 10cc would have dared to be so wry and avant-garde.

Did we need a second wall? For although *The Final Cut* is not *The Wall*, it is, by design and by accident, a sequel we did not need to that first exposition of Waters' imagination.

By the time of the film of *The Wall* (one of the greatest of film adaptations) and preparations for a new album, relationships within the group were more than just strained. Rick Wright had long ago been forced to resign, but, kept on as a paid session musician for the tour, he managed to get the last laugh in financial form. Roger Waters then assumed full control of the group, and David Gilmour struggled with that. Nick Mason found himself somewhere in the middle, remaining a friend of Waters through thick and thin. It looked very much as though Pink Floyd was about to implode.

As many have observed, *The Final Cut* is in effect a Waters solo album. There is some Gilmour guitar and Mason made some nice sounds, but the absence of Wright is like the proverbial elephant in the room, while Gilmour's solos are proficient – not the usual description of his playing. Waters created the concept, wrote the music and lyrics, and directed the whole thing, with help from co-producers James Guthrie and Michael Kamen, having the gall to complain to Gilmour that he had not contributed anything when Gilmour remarked that some of the material was below par. It was all a step too far. The album had been intended at first as a soundtrack to the film of *The Wall*, but the advent of the Falklands War changed Waters' concept. This was to be a work of bitter social comment and anti-war sentiment.

The album opened with *The Post War Dream*, which has a half-decent melody, carried by Waters' frail voice and a keyboard part. The brass instrumentation gave the track a slightly nostalgic feel, while the lyrics referred to Margaret Thatcher – Maggie, as all those who loathed her would say – and shipbuilding. But perhaps Waters should have left references to shipbuilding to Elvis Costello and, a little later, to Robert Wyatt. This song asked what Maggie had done to England and wondered what the correct response should be, yet the tone lacked irony, the lyrics lacked subtlety, and the vibe was somewhat grey.

Your Possible Pasts was another slow song, again with a fair melody. This was a song from the sound-world of *The Wall*, in vibe and content. A plea for closeness and empathy, its hits against religion found their mark. The Gilmour solo that accompanied it however, was most noticeable for the fact that, yes, it did sound like him. Yet in those Gilmour-esque flourishes could be heard a tone of half-disguised boredom. This was David Gilmour acting out the role of David Gilmour.

One Of The Few opened with a ticking clock before the arrival of a piano and guitar. Another frail vocal carried the lyrics, wherein lay a clever reference to George Orwell's *1984* in its "two plus two" line. This was a song about the delusions of authoritarianism, for which soldiers have to die. *The Hero's Return* was another track akin to *The Wall*, with a good melody and a dramatic production – excellent guitar and drum sounds. This was certainly a highlight of the album, and one of the few songs whose sounds, synthesisers and overall production succeeded on their own terms. Images of post-war celebrations in 1945 evoked the joy at the end of a gruelling conflict. *The Gunner's Dream* however, evoked darker themes: nuclear fallout, set to the sounds of a car and its radio. It was in effect a song of farewell, a Falklands song, whose incongruous saxophone solo ruined what little sparkle the piece had.

Paranoid Eyes continued the decline with music that was at best average. Lacking a tune, its lyrics described withdrawal into a world lurking behind a paranoid gaze. It was a song that tried to balance resistance and concealment, its sound effects of normal people on normal streets doing normal things balanced by hints of the brave face, of the mask, of lurking and danger. The brass accompaniment sounded out of kilter with these lyrics, trying to suggest the post-war world, yet invoking through its average arrangement little of note. There was an emptiness to this song that spoke of the anger and distress being felt by the three members remaining in the group. It sounded as though even Waters had given up trying.

Get Your Filthy Hands Off My Desert began with a missile and an explosion, its string quartet and sounds of distant aeroplanes evoking the many times authoritarian leaders have grabbed land from people living far away. References to the Falklands War were present. *The Fletcher Memorial Home* did not have much of a tune, featured the brass section again, and was rather slow and dull. As its accompanying video made clear, this song was about a home for retired political leaders, in which the likes of Hitler, Churchill, Maggie and others lurked like the solid ghosts of history. Many of these individuals were colonialists, the implication being that Maggie, herself, if not as a representative of British history, was one too. She, after all, had sent her soldiers eight thousand miles to the southern hemisphere to take back land grabbed from its owners a century and a half before. A Gilmour solo reminded the listener that this was a Pink Floyd album. *Southampton Dock* also lacked a tune, its half-sung, half-spoken lyrics describing soldiers boarding their ship, with crowds waving at their young sons and all the usual ceremony that accompanies such events. Mention of the Cenotaph, soldiers' graves and poppy fields rammed the point home.

The Final Cut continued this tuneless style. Waters had, for the album, accentuated his tortured vocal, which tried to emphasise emotional suffering but which in most cases came across as laboured to the extent of being embarrassing. This song was the worst offender. Against music vaguely reminiscent of *Comfortably Numb* with its competent guitar solo, it meandered this way and that. Gilmour, however, now became more visible, as *Not Now John* featured him singing and a vibe straight out of *The Wall*. Indeed, it recalled the rock mode of the song *Young Lust,* which Gilmour had made his own three years earlier. This song however, was pretty dire, with an inappropriate girly chorus and a Gilmour-standard solo. Lacking melody and heart, it was positioned in the track order in a place giving it the least perceived worth. The final track on *The Final Cut* was *Two Suns In The Sunset*. This song, in waltz-time and also tuneless, was a slow dirge about a nuclear fireball.

And that was it. The last song on the final Pink Floyd album. Although Waters' heart was in the right place with his subject matter, the LP vibe was grim, the music bearable at best, and the overall tone depressing. That the arrangements and execution were so humdrum spoke both of the implosion of the group and the paucity of imagination shown by those who created it. *The Final Cut* mentioned shipbuilding, but it was no *Shipbuilding*.

It is instructive to scroll through comments made online by Pink Floyd fans when it comes to this album. For myself, I disliked it when I heard it upon release, and I loathe it now. To me, it simply is not a Pink Floyd album. It is a Roger Waters whinge, whose early intentions may have been genuine and whose original concept had much promise, but which got lost amidst a maelstrom of thwarted creativity and self-righteousness.

Many other commentators agree, but, as is always the case, many fans disagree. But the comments made by fans are suggestive of the main problem here. Those against speak of the album being "so depressing it's unlistenable," "tripe," "doesn't even sound like Pink Floyd and is all about the lyrics," "has no redeeming qualities," and is in essence "songs rejected from *The Wall*," and a "Roger Waters therapy session." Those in favour speak of "great themes to this and *The Wall*," of the album being "strong and extraordinary," of "some good tracks," and of the LP being "a favourite."

The overall tone however, is clear. Waters is described as too dominant even by the yeasayers, while almost every other comment speaks of the loss of Rick Wright; that he was the soul of the group, that his absence "really shows." One fan simply said: "Needs more Gilmour."

The end was nigh. A fifteen-year run was over. As the soul of Pink Floyd sang it almost ten years before: *The song is over, thought I'd something more to say…*

Chapter 15

A Momentary Lapse Of Reason

ouseboats can be dark, dank and scuzzy, but not *Astoria*. Moored on the Thames in an exclusive mooring place, David Gilmour's houseboat had windows that sparkled in sunlight. Inside lay a small recording studio. There, as the 1980s reached their middle years, Gilmour, Mason and Wright gathered to test out new pieces of music and put together an album. Originally, some of the music had been intended for Gilmour's third solo album following the success of *About Face*, but now, with Roger Waters gone, it was time to reconsider the meaning of Pink Floyd. There would be new contributors too, some of them famous already, individuals with whom Gilmour had worked, or knew personally. He was ringing the changes.

Waters had stepped away from the group, but Gilmour made it plain to him that he intended carrying on beneath that awe-inspiring name; and even if Wright could not be named one-third of the group, he would be present as a session musician. These were the declarations and the stakes. All high.

There would be other changes. Since *The Dark Side Of The Moon*, there had been a founding concept for every Pink Floyd album. This time, whatever arrived at the end of recording and mixing would be a *collection* of songs, their own meaning, without a unifying banner and presented to fans under their own steam.

Gilmour not only had a boat, he had a boatman, Langley Iddins. The sound of Iddins rowing along the Thames opened the new album, in a piece co-written with Bob Ezrin called *Signs Of Life*. With fluttering synthesisers, those found sounds, and then a melodic theme and a chord sequence, the new Pink Floyd was announced. It was similar to the old, but everything yet remained to be revealed. But there was reinvigorated confidence here, perhaps founded in the keyboards of Rick Wright, who contributed to this opening track, that suggested many good things to come. The synthesisers sounded modern, especially that eerie, whistling timbre. The guitar harmonics, the tune and the solo which followed were all great. There were signs of life in the old 1970s behemoth.

But Gilmour was not only stepping off land to place himself upon water; he and Mason also had their gazes raised upwards. With both of them learning to fly, the first song proper celebrated that ambition. *Learning To Fly* was mid-paced, based on drum machine samples and razor-sharp guitars. Written with the assistance of Ezrin, Jon Carin and Anthony Moore, Gilmour sang of his aerial ambition, with Mason later providing air-coms voices to emphasise the mood and technology. Guitar riffs, a solo in classic Gilmour mode, then the arrival of soulful backing vocals added to the vibe. This was similar to the mood and timbres presented in *About Face,* but there was a hint of the old Pink Floyd in this dramatic new number, mostly found in the vocal arrangement. Gilmour, Mason and Wright had not found themselves short of inspiration. Mason's aeroplane intercom messages – *Check!* – and the memorable tune, scything guitar sound and modern production all contributed to an excellent opener. There was no metaphor here, no Roger Waters reference or allusion to death, just enthused descriptions of the delights of the airborne life as experienced by an "earthbound misfit." These were the pursuits of the privileged, but the sentiments were genuine.

The Dogs Of War seemed at first to echo the opening of *Animals,* with its strange, transformed snarls, but it soon veered off that course, as martial synthesisers and percussive effects led the listener into the track. The lyrics were sung with precision and conviction by Gilmour, again aided by a female backing vocal arrangement which added much to the overall vibe. The song's title was taken from Shakespeare's *Julius Caesar* – let slip the dogs of war – and concerned the trade of mercenaries, who have no cause except their own love of money and violence, and who consider the world to be their own boys' playground. Cash transfers, long-distance phone calls and luxurious living were their signals. A swirling Hammond keyboard harked back to 1970s sounds, and there were a lot of progressive-styled changes of tempo and rhythm in this song, especially when the drum enhanced guitar part gave way to a saxophone solo. Although these elements fitted naturally into the arrangement, by design or otherwise, they evoked memories of the old Floyd, especially that sax, at once chiming out the intentions of the new with reference to the old. It was a successful and striking synthesis.

Gilmour wrote the next song with his friend Phil Manzanera of Roxy Music. *One Slip* was the first track on the album to sound unlike classic Pink Floyd. In its opening synthesiser ambience, "warning" sounds, and then drum machine pattern twinned with more synthesisers, it sounded a little like some of Peter Gabriel's adventurous solo music, at the time commercially massive as well as lauded in reviews. The quick tempo hinted at something ominous, perhaps even dangerous. The song, when it arrived, was accompanied by mesmerising delayed guitars, its Gabriel-esque sound confirmed by the presence of bassist Tony Levin playing the Chapman Stick, then a novel and little-known instrument, but one too distinctive to be lost in the mix. The song's tempo, striking bridge with its whispered voices, and its open, freewheeling melody made it a standout track, the driving chorus and backing vocals relaying the album's title to the listener in thrilling form. With those new bass sounds, the conspicuous absence of Waters' voice, and dynamic arrangements, this was an experiment that worked in every department. Whether this song referred to a real encounter, an imaginary one, or more general concerns about the hazards of the touring life was unclear, but the narrator was "put to the test" – and it was all about mutual desire. One slip… a momentary lapse of reason… one regret.

On The Turning Away raised Gilmour's game even further. The standout track in an excellent album, it hinted at some of Paul McCartney's more folky melodies, such as that gracing *Mull Of Kintyre,* against which it could be favourably compared. Arranged with subtle acoustic guitar, synthesisers and drums, its lovely melody carried lyrics dealing with empathy, kindness and humility, with nods to the feelings everybody encounters upon death or at a funeral. Many Pink Floyd fans have had this song played at family funerals. As it reached out from wistfulness and elegy into a classic electric guitar and Hammond organ section, it spoke in universal terms to everyone listening, rightly remaining a classic of the Pink Floyd canon to this day. As Gilmour said in a December 1987 interview with *Only Music:* '*Turning Away* is about the political situations in the world. We have these rather right-wing conservative governments that don't seem to care about many things other than looking after themselves.' Gilmour's hope was that there would be no more turning away from the weak and the weary.

Yet Another Movie, written with Patrick Leonard, began with a synth drone, percussive effect samples, guitars and speaking voices. The saxophone and 1980s drum sound – plenty of snare reverb – propelled another great song, slow, confident, with a good melody. Gilmour's voice in particular sounded superb, echoed in creepy style by an accompanying vocal. Later, the much-used "blown bottle" sample and classic Gilmour guitar inserts took the song higher, with samples inserted from the films *One-Eyed Jacks* and *Casablanca: maybe not today, maybe not tomorrow…* A key change and doubled rhythm added to the sonic luxury of this progressive-sounding and memorable cut. The lyrics seemed to be about the life choices of ordinary people, especially in childhood, and how they related to the demons of adult life. Family relationships were implied in the first verse; adult problems in the second; then just the vacant look in the eyes of somebody whose life has run its course, and whose mind is full of regrets. Fading into the setting sun felt in this song like a metaphor for dying.

The synthesiser piece *Round And Around,* arranged in 5/4 time, followed, augmented by a guitar part. At one minute and thirteen seconds, it was a reverie designed to separate two sections of the album, the next part beginning with *A New Machine (Part 1).* This also short track was arranged for vocal and vocoder, its title evoking 1975, the vocoder 1977. Yet its sound was brand new, the lyrics speaking of weariness, of life and death inside a body – life as yourself, with so many possibilities which cannot be explored as the years, then the decades, pass by. It's only a lifetime… At just one minute and forty-seven seconds, this track segued into *Terminal Frost,* an instrumental in which the Gilmour sound dominated, yet which was entirely Floydian. Mid-paced, using a 1980s drum sound, with a striking piano riff and whirling guitars, its solos soared even as its rhythm track remained terrestrial. Drum machine samples, a soulful female backing chorus, a rippling saxophone solo and more spoken samples – *Never again…* – augmented a full, but not over-full arrangement. *A New Machine (Part 2)* bookended the track as its twin had.

This fine album concluded with *Sorrow,* a track which, unusually for Gilmour, came with lyrics first. The opening phrases, adapted from John Steinbeck's classic novel *The Grapes Of Wrath,* led into a mourning for a lost paradise to which the narrator was bound by ties of necessity. Frightened by this intense relationship, the narrator received no solace as he considered his life – even from the waters of the land, which, beneath smoke-shrouded skies, flowed on silent and regardless into a glutinous, bitter ocean. Over a bassy synthesiser drone, Gilmour laid a heavy guitar solo, its dense sound part guitar, part industrial implement. Guitar effects led into the song proper, its tune fair, not striking, but up to the task in hand, and underpinned by a terrific chord sequence. Stacked vocals and a change of key dramatized the chorus, which sounded quite different to the verse. Gilmour led the outro via his guitar once again.

There was a lot of David Gilmour on this album, but it was not a Gilmour solo LP, as *The Final Cut* had been a Waters solo. Collective effort, open minds, and joint musical composition aboard the houseboat all led to a work fit to be announced to the public under the name Pink Floyd. It did sound a little like *About Face* in places, but, just as *The Piper At The Gates Of Dawn* had been led by Syd Barrett, and the 1970s albums by Roger Waters, this was a Pink Floyd led by David Gilmour, who had every right to be there. It was born from his vision, with Rick Wright and Nick Mason both present.

To further cement the legitimacy of the brand, the cover design for the LP was created by Storm Thorgerson at Hipgnosis. Featuring a long line of hospital beds, the final image combined the use of real objects and photography, as had been the case with *Animals* almost a decade before. This support for the surreal Pink Floyd album cover was much appreciated by the fans. Reviewers, however, were split over the album's appeal and worth. Released in autumn 1987, two years after Waters' departure, some commentators felt it lacked bite, with lyrics not so incisive as before. But others saw the album's virtues, not least that after some time, the music was in true balance with the lyrics. That Pink Floyd were exploring and challenging the listener was evinced by a mention of the production values and lyrics of the two-part *A New Machine*.

Inside the original LP, for the first time in a decade and a half, there was a group photograph: Gilmour and Mason, both with big smiles on their faces. Wright, owing to legal issues, was only mentioned by name. But the message of the artwork was clear. Pink Floyd had returned.

Chapter 16

The Division Bell

By 1994, the era of CDs, begun not too long before the release of *A Momentary Lapse Of Reason,* was well underway. Yet the opening sounds of the brand new Pink Floyd album sounded faulty; noise, strange sounds, with nothing musical for the listener to get hold of. Was this a fault of the new laser-guided format?

No. It was the beginning of *Cluster One.*

Upon inspection, *The Division Bell* had all the hallmarks of a Pink Floyd release, not least the cover image, which was a photograph of a real object, a sculpture showing two separated semi-faces that at the same time composed one. David Gilmour was again at the helm, with Nick Mason and Rick Wright very much on the scene. But there were new names too, including bassist Guy Pratt. Dick Parry was still around playing the saxophone. Things were looking good.

Cluster One moved on from its spacey opening (which turned out to be electromagnetic noise from the solar wind) to an oscillating synthesiser sound, then a piano, a guitar, and a chord sequence. As the piece developed, it revealed itself through hints of percussion and a sequencer ostinato that rippled by. The addition of a Hammond organ and a piano-led theme brought the conclusion, the piece functioning as an album opener in the style of *Signs Of Life.*

The first song proper, *What Do You Want From Me?* featured drums, synthesiser bass and a funky keyboard, all wrapping up lyrics which, as on the rest of the album, had communication as their theme; and there was a new voice on some of these lyrics, Gilmour's partner Polly Samson, who would continue to work with Gilmour through his later solo career. David Gilmour had always been influenced by the blues. Supported by singers Durga McBroom, Sam Brown and Claudia Fontaine, the lyrics to this song described the painful source and consequences of singing or playing the blues – a musical form emerging from suffering and oppression. The second verse exposed the poverty of many artist/audience relationships, decorated with unfulfilled promises, with the conclusion a list of despairing options, including selling your soul. And in the end, is complete control what it has come to in this relationship? For this track, the production was excellent – sharp, precise, digital. The backing vocals emphasised the better chorus tune.

The opening 6/4 guitar part for *Poles Apart* sounded a little like Steve Hackett's song *Narnia* from his classic album *Please Don't Touch*, though here accompanied by Pratt's evocative fretless bass and Wright's trusty Hammond. That keyboard supported a great track with a strong melody, showing Gilmour's continuing ability with a tune. Again, the sonic quality was superb, emphasising the key change into the instrumental section, and then a woozy, dream-like part a little reminiscent of the fairground section from The Beatles' *Being For The Benefit Of Mr Kite*, with its waltz-time arrangement and trippy sonic effects. Yet when the song reappeared and a guitar solo began, all was returned to Floyd. David Gilmour, a sensitive man, was not unmoved by the traumas that visited themselves upon the group. So the lyrics of the first verse related to him having to take the position of Syd Barrett, and the guilt he felt about this. For the Cambridge men of the group, Syd was the gold-hued man, whose unique songs delighted the world. The second verse addressed a trauma no less awful, but which presented a veneer of bitterness, not tragedy. This was a verse about the departure of Roger Waters. The most significant line ran: *Did you know all the time, but it never bothered you anyway.* Here Gilmour refers to a facet of Waters' character that is perhaps misinterpreted; his deliberation when it comes to vandalism, argument and pride. And Gilmour describes himself from the other side, staring out the hard, impenetrable steel in Waters' gaze. I feel that this is a courageous song, a decade on from the group fracturing and a decade before that strange, surreal reunion for Live Aid. In the final verse, Gilmour seemed to make peace with the loss of Syd Barrett, to come to a melancholy resolution of all that heartache.

Marooned featured new technology, utilised by Gilmour to great effect, and was a track created from various part-improvised recordings. Opening with seagulls and seashore waves, its most striking feature was the octave-scale pitch bends created by the DigiTech Whammy Pedal, whose frequency-bending effects could be extreme. But every guitar part on this award-winning track (it received a Grammy) was exceptional, with Gilmour pulling out all the stops. Supported by piano and synthesisers, and half way through the drums coming in, it was classic Floyd from beginning to end, with the descending/ascending piano chords at the conclusion making a satisfying coda.

A Great Day For Freedom opened with Gilmour singing over a piano, harmony vocals arriving with synthesisers and tambourine. But this track moved on to epic territory, with drums and lush orchestration as the new chorus began. Meant to be anthemic and inspirational, its lyrical touchstones were liberty and rights, and it built and built as Gilmour played another epic guitar solo and the orchestration deepened. Gilmour told *The Sun* in September 2008 about this song, which was written by him and his wife, Polly: 'That song is really about the aftermath of the fall of the totalitarian state. First, it was a joy and a release for the people with the freedom of democracy but then it became horribly marred by the ethnic cleansing and genocide, particularly in Yugoslavia.' Gilmour spoke of friends and neighbours turning away from one another, the lack of repair to such relationships a cause for bitter regret.

Rick Wright was an official member of the group for this album. On *A Momentary Lapse Of Reason*, he could only be listed, since there was legal uncertainty in 1987 as to who exactly Pink Floyd could embrace when it came to core membership. The song *Wearing The Inside Out* was written and sung by him. That vocal was a first take, too. Underpinned by light synthesisers and percussion, there was also guitar and saxophone, hinting at arrangements for some of the songs on his solo album *Wet Dream*. The personal lyrics were classic Wright (the word "I" used a lot), carried by a great melody and the welcome return of that slightly frail, perhaps even querulous voice. Although Wright wrote the music for this track, the lyrics were written by Gilmour collaborator Anthony Moore. They described the return to the land of the living by a survivor of tragedy or trauma, who yearned for the night and who could hardly compose himself. Yet, in the end, he did survive, as mental clouds parted and he began to hear the world again. This was a song recognising something painful placed in the distant past. Backing vocals, the addition of Gilmour singing, and a female-led chorus beefed up the vocal arrangement, and there was even a synthesiser solo, now rare on a

Pink Floyd track. But the fans had missed that voice and those synthesiser sounds. On YouTube for this album, Wright's song has the second-highest viewing statistics after *Coming Back To Life*, indicating the regard he is held in by those who continue to love Pink Floyd.

A delayed guitar and keyboards opened the next track, *Take It Back*, whose euphoric melody was carried to perfection by Gilmour. Relationships as described through natural imagery informed this radio-friendly song: rain and waves, breath and breeze, the tale of a man and a woman. Yet the narrator of the lyrics was insecure. He could not help being suspicious. And he tested his partner, in doing so, damaging her. Yet this threatened the relationship – when love and faith turned into lies. It is the implicit loss of this relationship that fuelled the narrator's insecurity. He dared not relax.

Coming Back To Life featured a particularly gorgeous, undistorted guitar solo, and impassioned vocals later on, with the drums coming in half way through to ramp up the emotive effect. This was a song about reconnecting with life following the breaking of a relationship. They were amongst Gilmour's most personal and heartfelt lyrics: *I knew the moment had arrived, for killing the past and coming back to life.*

Keep Talking was a little bit different, featuring a voice alien to Pink Floyd yet amongst the most distinctive of the era. The synthesised voice of Stephen Hawking spoke on the topic of communication, following Gilmour seeing an advert for BT in which the great physicist spoke. With synthesisers aplenty, guitars and subtle percussion, the song yearned for full communication between people and between nations. With a backing chorus, a synthesiser solo, and a Frampton-style "talk box" guitar solo, the track was a production triumph.

Lost For Words complemented the track that preceded it, adding an anthemic chord structure and melody. This tune was good, as was the vocal that carried it. In a slightly deeper voice than usual, Gilmour sang about the value of empathy in communication and in life. The acoustic/electric guitar balance was pushed towards the former to excellent effect, with an acoustic solo at the end. Yet this song was not just about communication, for it was Gilmour's word on his relationship with Roger Waters. The lyrics were not hard to decipher: *Can you see your days blighted by darkness? Is it true you beat your fists on the floor? Stuck in a world of isolation, while the ivy grows over the door.*

The final track on this album has gone down in legend as one of Gilmour's – and thus Pink Floyd's – finest. *High Hopes* is consistent in its significance to fans worldwide. A song of hope with lyrics rooted in Gilmour's Cambridge childhood, it opened with church bells, then a piano against a sampled bell. A great melody underpinned themes of home and leaving it, with a strings-augmented lap steel solo to conclude. The affecting beauty of the song has impressed itself upon millions of listeners, with many finding it one of the most meaningful in the entire Pink Floyd canon. Although there are references to the early days of the group planted into the lyrics by Gilmour and Polly Samson, the song itself, which is autobiographical, is not specifically about the group. And just as the first song on Pink Floyd's first album featured the voice of their then manager Peter Jenner, so the concluding part of this song featured a recording of current manager Steve O'Rourke. It was a masterful touch.

There were a few naysayers upon release, but most reviewers found this album both rewarding and an artistic success. It had a theme, unlike its predecessor, one delivered with subtlety.

Chapter 17

The Endless River

Richard Wright died of lung cancer in September 2008, aged 65. The Floyd world mourned. This was the soul of the group gone forever. *The Endless River* was released to bring back his magic touch one last time.

The Endless River was based upon music recorded during sessions for *The Division Bell,* with some of the construction work occurring during the two years prior to the album's release. Originally an hour-long mix by Andrew Jackson entitled *The Big Spliff,* it was recorded in various locations, including at Britannia Row Studios and on David Gilmour's houseboat, and it merged music not originally intended for release with new compositions, Gilmour and Mason working with known collaborators such as Bob Ezrin and Jon Carin. Gilmour's friend Phil Manzanera from Roxy Music also piloted some of the early work, including the arrangement into four suites. Almost entirely instrumental, the album featured compositions which some critics called meandering or uninspired, but which on closer inspection revealed an understanding of subtlety and the power of the ambient genre to evoke quieter, less "rock" emotions. There was no hard-hitting concept, little by way of strident guitars or powerful drums, yet the whole, when appreciated over time and with the perspective of the whole career of the group, achieved a subtle power unlike any previous release.

In 2010, that understated power was featured on an album by The Orb entitled *Metallic Spheres.* Having remixed an online single, *Chicago – Change The World,* by David Gilmour, Alex Paterson and Youth of The Orb asked Gilmour to provide some new guitar parts. In due course, an entire album expanded and reworked from original material was created. The Orb had for almost two decades led the way through the complex, glittering world of ambient music, Paterson's influences visible not least via the Battersea Power Station image depicted on the *Adventures Beyond The Ultraworld* album. But the construction of complex music – electronic progressive with touches of psychedelia and techno – was as much a legacy of Pink Floyd's presence in the world as that famous image.

If the music for *The Endless River* was subtle, even restrained, its cover design was pure Pink Floyd. Storm Thorgerson died in 2013 as the music was being created, but the image of a man boating along fluffy clouds, created by Stylorouge in association with Aubrey Powell of Hipgnosis, was perfect for the mood: elegiac, wistful, dreamy through floating. It captured the end of a long journey, one during which battles had been fought, mountains ascended, every obstacle overcome. The man on the boat had his back to the viewer – we cannot see his face. It is either Richard Wright or somebody representing him. It was an image of farewell, one in which an unknown far distance is the destination. On the rear of the release, the boat was depicted empty, its oars set akimbo, while it sat motionless.

Things Left Unsaid opened in ambient style, its voices and shimmering synthesisers, beautifully recorded, with more than a hint of The Orb. New higher-pitched synthesisers came in to bring a weightless feeling, matching the atmospheric cover image. There were hints too of Eno's ambient explorations in the sparse, but gorgeous vibe. A treated guitar part was the final touch, its notes smoothed off into flowing phrases as the whirring chords underneath twisted and intertwined. Even if this track had been presented to the world by The Orb, it would still stand out.

The track segued directly into *It's What We Do,* which continued the vibe but added synthesiser parts from Rick Wright. The guitar and percussion underneath were mixed to perfection, and when the rhythm emerged, there was more than a hint of Wright's unforgettable work on *Wish You Were Here.* Gilmour's accompanying solo was understated to perfection. This was a true duet, not an artefact of the mixing desk, which, given the circumstances, was quite an achievement. There was also a hint of *Animals* in the electric piano sound. What was remarkable about Gilmour's solo is that it could have been over the top, but it was not. With classic Wright string sounds and that whirring Hammond organ, it evoked the Pink Floyd past to perfection. It was a gorgeous piece of music that recalled and celebrated not only Wright but the classic 1970s sounds. A direct segue into *Ebb And Flow* took the rhythm out, leaving just floating chords and wisps of ebow guitar. There were no vocals, just those marvellous instruments.

Sum opened with more spooky synthesisers, this time from Gilmour on the VCS3, oscillating to a faster rhythm. A full band piece then began, this time with more of a "classic" Gilmour guitar sound, the keyboards rippling in the background. Again, although Gilmour did pull out his technical tricks, this was an emotive solo that fell short of bombastic tendencies. The accompanying synthesisers matched it to perfection, until, as the rhythm cut out, the music ascended into endless blue.

This piece segued into *Skins,* which was the most rock-sounding cut so far with its clattering percussion and driving bass. As with most of the music on this album, it was an instrumental, but there was so much going on, especially in Nick Mason's complex rhythms, the listener did not miss voices singing; and it certainly did not sound like filler.

Unsung returned the listener to shimmering keyboards that hinted again at The Orb, this time augmented by Wright's piano and a wailing guitar solo; not screeching, but dark and subtle. Only Wright and Gilmour played here – brothers in music once again. This segued straight into *Anisina,* in which drums, bass and the piano all featured. The music had an elegiac feel through its chord sequence, which darted off then swiftly resolved. Again, Gilmour kept his solo beautifully restrained, with superb clarinet (Gilad Atzmon) and saxophone entering the mix as the music swelled, the clearer, jazzier saxophone emerging for the breakdown.

The Lost Art Of Conversation was written by Wright alone, his music augmented by Gilmour. In its soft subtlety, it recalled old age – a kind of wisdom through sound. The listener could imagine those two familiar faces, lined and framed in white hair… *On Noodle Street* followed without a break, its rhythm and bass supporting Wright's classy Fender Rhodes part. There seemed so little to this track on first hearing, but that bass and Jon Carin's synthesisers kept the listener's attention. Another direct segue took the listener into *Night Light,* which matched Gilmour's ebow guitar with Wright's similarly dreamlike synthesisers.

Allons-y (1) sounded like 1980s-era Pink Floyd, with Gilmour's guitar solo more akin to those he recorded at the time. It is a solo Gilmour composition that led directly into *Autumn '68,* a title echoing Wright's song *Summer '68.*

Here, he played the Royal Albert Hall pipe organ, with Mason providing a supporting gong part. Gilmour, meanwhile, followed the melody played by Wright, augmenting it here and there. Then *Allons-y (2)* returned, with more Floydian guitar parts and a hint of the delayed sound employed so well on *The Wall*. Here, the contrasts between the song parts fitted well.

Talkin' Hawkin' was perhaps the misstep of the album, in that it used Stephen Hawking's voice (and Gilmour's for the backing vocals), with Durga McBroom adding a soulful extra voice. It was pretty much the same sentiment as on *The Division Bell,* which seemed a bit of a shame in the context.

The last of the four main sections on this album opened with the eerie synthesisers of *Calling,* another fine piece of ambient construction created by Gilmour and his co-writer Anthony Moore. This led straight into *Eyes To Pearls,* which began with a spiky guitar riff before filling out with the addition of gong, bass and percussion. The details of the music here were restrained, but that added to the atmosphere of tension, which dissipated the moment the acoustic guitar of *Surfacing* entered the mix. This was another Gilmour solo piece, a bridge between the music so far and the final song, *Louder Than Words,* performed in the main on guitars, with euphoric backing vocals ramping up the emotional content. Both Mason and Wright contributed to the music here.

Written by Gilmour and Polly Samson, this last ever Pink Floyd song began with an arpeggiated guitar and a piano sounding out a melancholic theme. Gilmour's vocal recalled the fights and struggles of the group, and there was no doubt that it was sung with absolute conviction. There was age in those deeper, rougher vocal tones. The backing vocals and, later, string section arrangement gave a suitably anthemic feel to this farewell song, which concluded with an eerie melding of synths and sounds – saying goodbye to Wright's keyboards. The melody was memorable, with a simple but strong chord sequence. This song was inspirational enough to close both the album and the group's career. On its multiple shoulders, the legacy of the group was set free into the sky, drifting on a simple, shallow boat along the endless river.

I think Richard Wright would have been pleased with this album, perhaps even proud. It was a tribute to him: an elegy. As such, it did not feature the progressive fireworks of classic-era Pink Floyd, nor the cunning wordplay and psychedelic effects of the Syd Barrett era. The distinctive guitar sounds heard on such albums as *The Wall, About Face* and *The Division Bell* were muted, softened by digital effects and the ebow mode of playing. This chilled sound world was a metaphor for the end of life; of its quietness, its propensity for reflection, its inclination to think back, to evaluate and above all to remember. Some keyboard sounds were like chinks of light illuminating the past: *Wish You Were Here,* for instance, which Wright made such a contribution to. Elsewhere, the ability of the man to play was celebrated.

Like David Gilmour, Wright preferred to play music without too much deliberation. If, for Gilmour, a guitar was a way to express his feelings, for Wright, a keyboard was a channel through which something – he did not need to know what – might emerge. He was an intuitive player, comfortable with feel, vibe and improvisation, which is why he was attracted to jazz in the early days. His grasp of melody allowed something unique to manifest in the group when he was there. And Gilmour was his companion through music. The two men shared an intuitive bond, present in the twin vocals of *Echoes,* which for so many is Pink Floyd's most beloved song, but also manifested through twin creations of guitar strings and synthesisers. Some have suggested that Wright was the soul of the group, but it might be worth adding that Wright and Gilmour together were that entity – the musical heart. For all Waters' undoubted brilliance with concepts and lyrics, the two musical titans were the X factor; inexplicable, mysterious, something to experience and luxuriate in, not to try to break down into pieces.

Gilmour and Mason were in effect contributing players on this album, with Wright centre stage on many tracks. Yet as a whole, the piece was unalloyed Floyd. Phil Manzanera, producing, wanted to evoke all eras of the group, exploring their quintessential sound – the entire canon. In achieving this, *The Endless River* also brought closure to one of the most remarkable stories in rock music. This was not a yearning for the past, rather an acceptance of it.

All the great groups in pop and rock live and progress because the whole is greater than the sum of the parts. Pink Floyd breathed. Pink Floyd grew and created.

Chapter 18

Pompeii MCMLXXII

It all began as a request to David Gilmour and the group's manager, Steve O'Rourke, in the first half of 1971 from a film director, but not about the fabulous Roman amphitheatre ruins. Adrian Maben wanted to match Pink Floyd's music with surreal art images, including famous images made by René Magritte. This suggestion was rejected, however. Shortly afterwards, Maben went on holiday to Italy, and in due course found himself at the ruins of Pompeii, destroyed when the volcano Vesuvius erupted almost two thousand years earlier. As he walked the area and surveyed the site, he began to have ideas of filming once again with the group, but live this time. The Pompeii environment, quiet, ancient, unique, would be an extraordinary place to film a concert, one befitting a remarkable group.

A contact at the University of Naples, who happened to be a massive Floyd fan, led to success. The whole site could be closed for six days in October of that year. The gamble had paid off, albeit after the handing over of a lot of money.

Still, much remained to be prepared. The group told Maben they would only play live. There would be no audience, reversing the recent trend for music films. Only the group's crew and filming technicians would see and hear. (In the end, a few children did sneak in to listen.)

Between 4 and 7 October, various songs from the group's current repertoire were filmed. The group, O'Rourke and Maben chose suitable tracks, the latter particularly interested in *A Saucerful Of Secrets*. But songs from the new album *Meddle* were also on the table, not least the LP's opener *One Of These Days*.

There were logistical issues. Electricity came via a very lengthy cable. Setting up in such conditions was difficult. In the end, the longer tracks were filmed in sections, with approval sessions following each part. Maben also filmed volcanic mud and the group wandering around the site.

Two months later, filming concluded at a Parisian studio. And constraints continued, leading eventually to Maben having to finish up editing under his own steam in his own home.

September 1972 saw the film premiere, by which time *Meddle* was old and *The Dark Side Of The Moon* was on the way. At that time, the film ran for only an hour – just the live footage. Subsequent versions included later studio footage relating to *The Dark Side Of The Moon*.

In May 2025, a set of remastered versions was released, and this included, for the first time, a CD of the audio.

The CD opens with a foreboding of 1973 in the form of a heartbeat: the *Pompeii Intro*. The film, in its later versions, included excerpts of the group working in the recording studio on *The Dark Side Of The Moon*, and this introduction, complete with swirling synthesisers and cymbals, evokes the opening of that album.

Echoes – Part 1, which comprises the first two sections, opens the event. At the time of filming this epic piece of music had yet to be released on the *Meddle* LP, which would not come out until the following month, recording sessions for the album having concluded the previous month. The group were well aware that *Echoes* might be a cornerstone of their future; the song had to be included. This live version includes all the song's components, albeit stripped down to the essentials. But it is a remarkable partner to the studio version, its elements in no way inferior. Gilmour's guitar opening in particular, with that sliding, gliding quality created by the gliss technique, is wholly in tune with Wright's slowly evolving piano part. When the bass and drums enter the mix and the full guitar opens out, it is a marvellous moment, which then moves on to a particularly gorgeous slide guitar solo.

As with the studio version, Gilmour and Wright take the vocals, with Wright's harmony vocal somehow elegiac in tone, the differing quality of the men's voices somehow more apparent than in the perfectly fused studio version. Nevertheless, it is a flawless take of that unforgettable melody. And when Gilmour's second solo comes in, wreathed in fuzz, it really does leap into the Pompeii skies – soaring in majesty.

The funky section emphasises Wright's mastery of the Hammond organ, which whirrs and stamps underneath Gilmour's second soaring solo. Again, these two musicians play in harmony, with Waters and Mason especially (his drum sound is excellent) providing a tight and solid backing. Yet it is Gilmour's unique guitar that carries the section, including many of his signature sounds which would in later years come to signify his position in the pantheon of rock guitarists. Roger Waters marks the end of this recording with a bass flurry.

Careful With That Axe, Eugene again shows off the interplay between Gilmour and Wright, as Gilmour's plaintive guitar, supported by his wordless vocalisations, slips and slides around Wright's mournful keyboards. Waters' vocal part in this version is much more expansive than in other versions, with hisses and whispers in the mix, as well as a few almost-screams before the main scream… which, when it arrives, is full of pain and horror. Waters also spells out the full title just before: Careful with that axe, Eugene! Gilmour repeats his own vocalisations as his impassioned solo progresses. This is one of the best versions of this live classic yet to be officially released. It is full of the psychic terror and creeping horror that the group wished to evoke. When the second, quieter Waters vocal comes in, it sounds like the last breaths of a dying man, alone and mentally devastated in some archaic mausoleum.

A Saucerful Of Secrets is presented in two versions on this release, one unedited and about two and a half minutes longer. Both show the critical role of Nick Mason in the track. The opening cosmic section is suitably floaty, with slide guitar effects bubbling up over cymbals; later on, the guitar and the cymbals crash in unison, before Mason's rhythm enters the mix – quite a bit faster than in other live versions. He increases the tempo as the section develops, with a *huge* Gilmour slide guitar screeching over the top, and Wright's atonal piano clashing, until, with Mason in full and fastest flow, the guitar reaches down into its lowest register and the section fades. A few echo and feedback guitar effects take over, with the rhythm now just a pattering underplay, until all that is left is Rick Wright and his melancholic keyboard.

The final section, which in the studio version is much more of a choral affair, is here, as with all the live versions, Gilmour alone taking the vocal part. In Pompeii, however, he does imbue the part with a lot of feeling, evoking something majestic; transcendent even. Yet we, the listeners, cannot know what that is. There are no words, just the vocal melody to indicate what secrets the music is conveying.

One Of These Days opens with Waters' immediately recognisable bass riff, before Mason comes in with splashy drums and cymbals, then Wright. This seems like quite a staid affair, until Gilmour makes his entrance with that half chainsaw, half blues guitar sound that characterises this piece. In the staccato section, there is much more by way of spiralling effects from Wright and Gilmour, with Mason brilliant underneath. Gilmour's closing solo pulls out a little more heavy blues from this thrumming, clashing instrumental.

Set The Controls For The Heart Of The Sun is here presented in epic format, opening with gongs and buzzing keyboards, before the pattering tom-tom rhythm emerges. This time, Wright echoes the melody before Waters comes in to sing. The admiration with which this song, composed by Waters alone, is still held indicates its exceptional quality. Waters' vocal here is weirdly querulous, as though presaging madness to come – quite a vocal performance from somebody who has on various occasions questioned his singing ability. When the song picks up tempo and Wright's solo, still distorted, begins to take flight, the music reaches an intensity befitting such a great piece. As with *A Saucerful Of Secrets,* the group increase the tempo at the end of the intense section, before a cosmic keyboard drop sets the mood for the final section. A great rendition, this, with Waters and Wright in particular setting the tone and mood, the latter with some superb cosmic synthesiser sounds.

Mademoiselle Nobs is a nod to *Seamus* from *Meddle,* in which a dog (on this occasion a Borzoi named Nobs belonging to Madonna Bouglione, the daughter of circus manager Joseph Bouglione) howls along to the group's bluesy little number.

Echoes – Part 2 concludes the main set, beginning with that unique combination of guitar screaming, bass ambience and crow caws. There can be little doubt that this section and the shimmering music which follows is amongst the most moving and evocative of all the group's output. Here, live and conveyed by just the four of them, it is as remarkable as ever. When the song returns, when Gilmour plays his final, heartbreaking solo, and when the ever-rising choir evokes vast blue skies, the listener can soar alongside Gilmour, Mason, Waters and Wright.

Pink Floyd fans now have a considerable catalogue of post-copyright live music to choose from, of which, for this book, I chose to focus on *The Broadcast Sessions.* But this remixed and remastered version of the fifty-five-year-old performance is one of the best sets I have ever heard. It shows a group on the cusp of true greatness, which would be theirs after six extraordinary years in which they did remarkable things, but explored a few blind alleys also. The signs are all here, emblazoned against the ancient pillars and stacks of Roman Pompeii.

Chapter 19

Redux, Gdansk & Secrets

It was announced to the astonishment of much of the rock music world. On the fiftieth anniversary of one of the greatest albums of all time, Roger Waters was going to release a reworked version of *The Dark Side Of The Moon. Redux,* it was called. That meant brought back, restored. He was going to rethink the whole album. And… people were going to have to listen to it.

Many voices asked the obvious questions. Why on earth was he doing it? What possible purpose could it serve? Had John Lennon, observing the small triumph of *Sgt. Pepper's Lonely Hearts Club Band,* later decided to record a better version, one which perhaps would not lean so much on Paul McCartney? Would Michael Jackson release an album entitled *Even More Thrilling* produced by John Leckie?

I was as baffled as everyone else, and appalled too. Even given that Waters was one of the master architects of the album, it was a concept so off the scale of taste and decency it circumvented even satire. There had to be a reason for him doing it. Later, I read the comments he made in support of his plan. These were given to *The Telegraph* newspaper, and were widely reported at the time. "I wrote *The Dark Side Of The Moon.* Let's get rid of all this 'we' crap. Of course we were in a band, there were four of us, we all contributed – but it's my project, and I wrote it."

What could have given rise to these comments, which for the majority of the group's fans must have verged on offensive? I certainly found them offensive. In this book, I have tried to be true and fair to all the members of Pink Floyd, acknowledging great talent and skill where it resided. Talent of high quality undoubtedly lay within Roger Waters. This was the man who wrote the best tunes on the *More* film soundtrack. This was the man who conceived *The Wall.* This was the man who wrote the line, "Two lost souls swimming in a fish bowl." Yet when I think of him now, I find a sneer on my lips and a feeling of revulsion in my mind. How did he fall so far in my estimation, and that of millions of fans elsewhere?

When I consider the overall thrust of popular and rock music from the 1950s, I notice a curious transformation around the turn of the millennium. Until then, especially in the 1960s and 1970s, but also through the next two decades, there was a premium on *melody* in rock and pop music. A song was not a song without a tune – preferably a stunner of a tune. And so, when people think of the greatest melodies in rock and pop, they think of *Stairway To Heaven*, they fondly recall the No. 1 smash hit *Everlasting Love* by Love Affair, they find themselves humming *Wuthering Heights* by Kate Bush, or they hear in their minds the twin vocals of David Gilmour and Rick Wright on *Echoes*. There were, of course, plenty of great melodies in the following two decades, but then, as the century turned and the influence of rap began to take hold, a strange and terrible thing happened. People began to equate songwriting with lyric writing.

I have wondered for a long time why this has happened. I find it disturbing. It is a little like those environmental "canaries in the mine", such as microplastics and coral reef bleaching, that make your skin crawl and a feeling of cold horror fall across you. Microplastics and coral bleaching are signs of a great wrong. I feel that the diminished position of melody in modern pop and rock music, the primacy of lyric writing, and the crass equating of songwriting with lyric writing are also canaries. These phenomena are telling us that something bad is happening in our music culture.

When Roger Waters, apparently without any sense of self-conscious reflection, or even wry amusement, told the world that he wrote *The Dark Side Of The Moon*, he might have felt that, because he came up with the ideas and the lyrics, that was what mattered. That, according to him, was not only the heart of the album but the only part worth concentrating on. Yes, there were contributions – such delightful contributions, made by men who played musical instruments in the same studio as him – but they were not what mattered. What was significant, and in the end the only thing worth restoring and rethinking in his *Redux*, was the words. And so, as if from the end of a slurry pipe emerging from a farm tank, he sprayed brown words over *Any Colour You Like*, one of the tracks that in the original version did not have his name attached. It is worth being reminded of those 1973 writing credits in full. They go as follows: Mason; Wright/Gilmour; Gilmour/ Waters; Mason/Waters/Wright/Gilmour; Wright/Torry; Waters; Wright; Gilmour/Mason/Wright; Waters; Waters.

Roger Waters believes that the concept and the lyrics are the only significant aspects of the album, and this is what allows him to make such absurd statements as, "It's my project and I wrote it." But there is more to *The Dark Side Of The Moon* than the words, or even the overarching idea. Like many other fans, I find the idea of "lyrics equals album" gross and repulsive. It is a matter of hideous irony that Waters, who wrote that "two plus two" lyric in his song *One Of The Few*, referring to George Orwell's *1984*, decided to rewrite the past in order to bring *Redux* to the attention of the world. The fact that he did not excise *Any Colour You Like* from *Redux* but instead wrote *new* words for it is evidence enough of his state of mind. Not only are the old words the crucial part of *The Dark Side Of The Moon*, but according to him, these brand new ones – which have nothing to do with the original conception – are just as important. That smacks of delusion. It is an attempt to rewrite, yes, but not the album. It is a rewrite of history. I am not alone in finding that contemptible.

Whether Waters is part of the strange and perturbing modern trend to equate songwriting with lyric writing, or whether it really is all about his bitter revenge on the album that propelled him into superstardom, is a moot point. Only those who know the man in person are qualified to answer it. Yet, in a book about Pink Floyd written by a man who loved, and still loves, the music and the glorious history of the group, we have to consider the question of Waters and his place in Pink Floyd.

It is common enough for band members to fall out with one another and bring one beloved musical edifice or another crashing to the ground. This has happened to many bands. It only did not happen to mine because there never really was a band, just me and the musicians I was working with at the time. But Pink Floyd was a real group, a true group in which the whole could be more than the sum of their parts, with world-class significance and millions of adoring fans.

Those fans have made many online memes about Pink Floyd, and one of the most interesting shows a photograph with all five members, each of them attached to a descriptive word. It goes as follows: David Gilmour, The

Voice; Syd Barrett, The Mind; Nick Mason, The Heartbeat; Roger Waters, The Face; Rick Wright, The Soul. I think this meme is of considerable interest when considering the relationship issues between the band members, notably Waters and Wright, and Waters and Gilmour. Waters is conceived of as the face of Pink Floyd, which in effect is its identity; and that, during much of the 1970s, was true enough, and no doubt celebrated by the rest of the group as their music and the success which followed began to reach all parts of the globe. Roger Waters *did* create the great overarching concepts of four amazing albums between 1973 and 1979. Yet look at how Gilmour and, in particular, Wright are conceived: the voice and the soul. This is as near as it is possible to saying they are the *music* of the group; its *emotional* heart. Wright, in particular, his loss mourned by innumerable fans after his ignominious ejection, is thought of as the soul of the group, which, whether you believe in such things or not, is tantamount to saying the one single entity that animates and gives life. That Gilmour, Wright's brother-in-music, should be characterised as the voice just adds more to this metaphor. Wright and Gilmour *are*, in essence, the music.

If Waters is the concept and the lyrics, what did he feel about being in the same group as two such extraordinary, natural, and above all, melodious musicians? As the dynamics changed when the spitting incident occurred, and as the first brick of the wall was set down, followed by the dysfunctional relationships of *The Wall* recording sessions, he found himself in conflict with Richard Wright – the *soul* of the group. A couple of years later, he found himself in conflict with David Gilmour, the *voice* of the group. Is it possible that in Waters' youth a tiny seed of envy was planted by the grim and tragic life experiences he endured, and that, when he achieved world recognition and the plaudits of millions, that envy began to grow, because it was nurtured, then to focus on the two things the fans said were best represented in Pink Floyd by Wright and Gilmour. For by the turn of that decade, a rebalancing had occurred, placing much greater emphasis on the lyrics – the thing Waters was genuinely brilliant at – over the music. As a consequence that music, represented by two of his group fellows, became less important, and the men with whom the music was associated were quarrelled with, then removed. Some observers of Pink Floyd, including myself in this book, have noted that Waters' technical musical talents were solid, if not spectacular. I think Waters must have been aware of all this as the group developed and success gave them everything they dreamed of. Pink Floyd became *important* on the world stage, and Waters could not allow that to continue out of his control. I think he demoted the importance of his fellow group members because he envied their natural ease with music. He, after all, was not so great.

There is, of course, another interpretation of that devastating line, "It's my project and I wrote it." It was Waters who, in 1985, left Pink Floyd. He removed himself from the group. Seeing that Gilmour in particular was not going to give up the legal fight, he separated himself from the monolith in order to reposition himself. That allowed him to devote himself to a solo career, but more importantly, it allowed him to attack Pink Floyd in a new way, should he wish to. What, then, if *Redux* was *intended* to soil the legacy of that classic album? Why should the embittered Waters care now in his old age about trouncing *The Dark Side Of The Moon?* What if he *wanted* to spray shit all over it? He, after all, in some eyes, would be the one man who could. Yet, judging by the reviews and fan responses, the majority of those who love Pink Floyd found his deed perplexing, distasteful and unnecessary. Yet Waters may not have found it so. He had nothing to lose, after all. He simultaneously promoted his own artistry with *Redux* and defiled *The Dark Side Of The Moon*, dressing it all up in terms of reinterpretation, of a new version for a new political generation and so forth. Yet for me at least, though I suspect also for innumerable others, the original album has been polluted by *Redux,* because we admired and respected Roger Waters back in the day, and because he did create the overarching structure and most of the lyrics of that classic LP. We cannot undo his membership of the group. But, alas, we do not want to. We are left in a tragic situation, tragic because it is out of our control – in the hands of the music gods. And the music gods decided to besmirch beauty.

I think Waters may have expected to be lambasted by the reviews of *Redux*. To be fair, a few reviewers, albeit in an uncertain tone of voice, said that some of the album was listenable, even interesting. But Waters, of all people in the world, was aware of the sheer scale and profundity of the monument that was created in 1973, and he knew that most would find his decision to re-record the songs objectionable. Many of the reviews (for instance, the superb one in *The Quietus*) did not pull their punches. But perhaps there was a grim and bitter smile on Roger Waters' face when he first came up with the idea, perhaps a long, chuckling snigger as he considered the fuss that would be generated by its release. Who knows?

By moving himself away from Pink Floyd, he gave himself free rein to do as he wished with the monolith and the legacy. It was a position of great power.

With great power comes great responsibility.

David Gilmour, meanwhile, continued to release excellent solo albums (especially *On An Island*) and play classic Pink Floyd numbers in his live sets.

The Gdansk concert took place in Gdansk Shipyard, the final date of the *On An Island* tour of 2006. Released in 2008, it was the last work to feature Rick Wright, who died just as the set was being released. Gilmour began his epic concert to a fifty-thousand-strong audience with four tracks from *The Dark Side Of The Moon: Speak To Me, Breathe, Time,* and the reprise of *Breathe.* As audience pleasers, these selections could not fail. The other Pink Floyd tracks came from *Wish You Were Here* and a broad range of early albums: *Astronomy Domine, Fat Old Sun, Echoes, Comfortably Numb* and *High Hopes.* All these songs feature high on lists of fan favourites, so their selection could be expected. *A Great Day For Freedom* from *The Division Bell* directly referenced the location of the concert, given that Gdansk was the birthplace of the Polish Solidarity trade union.

In choosing *Astronomy Domine,* Gilmour gave an appropriate nod to the earliest days of the group, as he did with *High Hopes,* while with *Echoes* he acknowledged the power of the pre-*Dark Side* material; and *Fat Old Sun* is as Gilmour-esque a song as could be imagined. Though he was promoting and celebrating his own solo work for the Gdansk concert, he could hardly play so prestigious an event without referencing the group. Nor did he feel that he had to. The glamour that arises from a quartet of musicians being greater than the sum of their parts would have sputtered and died without him. In choosing these tracks, Gilmour referenced his own essential part in that remarkable story. He did that with style and with fine judgement.

Gilmour is sometimes irritated by what aspects of his legacy are latched upon by the music press during interviews. He can be irritated by references to the departure of Roger Waters and the continuing feud between the two men, especially when (as with the release of *Luck And Strange* in 2024) he is trying to promote new work. But journalists always hunt for the human story, and the tale of Waters and Gilmour will never fade from the public's mind. That is one of the downsides of living a life partly in the public sphere.

In February 2022, the Ukrainian singer Andriy Khlyvnyuk recorded a version of the opening verse of the Ukrainian anthem *Oh, The Red Viburnum In The Meadow*, written over a century earlier by Stepan Charnetskii. Khlyvnyuk then filmed a performance of it in Sophia Square in Kyiv, which he posted on Instagram a few days later. This post came to the attention of Gilmour's daughter-in-law, the Ukrainian artist Janina Pedan, and it was this, together with the frustrations of witnessing on the news the unprovoked attack upon a peaceful independent country, that inspired Gilmour to sit up and think of something that he could do. That thing was to phone Nick Mason and suggest a collaboration under the Pink Floyd banner. Mason agreed, and with the support of Khlyvnyuk, the process began. On 30 March 2022, *Hey Hey Rise Up!* was recorded at Gilmour's home, with Gilmour and Mason in attendance alongside Guy Pratt and the renowned fusion and world music keyboard player Nitin Sawhney. Gala Wright, Rick Wright's daughter, also attended the session. The song opened with a sample from a recording of the anthem by the Veryovka Ukrainian Folk Choir. Received with praise and appreciation, the song in its physical formats was backed with the pro-peace song *A Great Day For Freedom*. Most music journalists and critics grasped the importance of using the Pink Floyd name for this gesture.

Alas, the release of the song on 8 April provoked Waters and a few fans to bemoan his and Wright's absence. There followed undignified assertions online, the most damaging of which was Waters' insistence in calling the attack "the most provoked invasion ever," claiming there was an anti-Russian stance across much of the West. With only the non-Waters Pink Floyd music stripped from Russian and Belarusian online music servers, the implication was that Waters had blocked taking down any music with which he had been involved. This spat spoiled some of what Gilmour and Mason had prepared, though the overall response was excellent, with the single hitting the charts and doing well in America. As for Andriy Khlyvnyuk, he made it plain that he thought the song was fabulous.

Of the three surviving members of Pink Floyd, it is perhaps Nick Mason who has best kept the group's flag flying high. While Roger Waters has released solo albums and other fare, as has David Gilmour, neither man has embraced the Pink Floyd back catalogue in quite the same way as Mason.

In 2018, following informal contacts from Floyd-loving musicians, Nick Mason – by then becoming a little tired of feeling like a figure from antiquity – decided to embrace the older music in a way nobody else had. Many of the group's fans whom he encountered knew the music from *The Dark Side Of The Moon* onwards very well, since the staggering sales of that album tended to obscure the smaller sales of earlier albums. The songs on *Atom Heart Mother*, for instance, or *A Saucerful Of Secrets*, were not so well known. Mason decided he wanted to highlight that music, but in an original way.

Soon enough, a band of five musicians was assembled. Alongside Mason stood guitarist Lee Harris, one-time member of The Blockheads, regular Pink Floyd associate and bassist Guy Pratt, Gary Kemp of Spandau Ballet on guitar and vocals, and synthesiser player Dom Beken. This quintet began rehearsing, whereupon the natural and easy-flowing quality of their music was recognised at once, not least by Mason himself. There was no intention of replicating the old group – Kemp was not to act in Syd Barrett's place – rather, the idea was to highlight the best of the early material and have some fun in the process. With successful rehearsals completed, the group performed a debut appearance at the Dingwalls Club in London, and then other British gigs. The vibe was good. The response was positive. Nick Mason's Saucerful Of Secrets was a going concern. This was no tribute act, rather it was an attempt, fuelled in the main by enthusiasm and love, to capture the emotional heart of those pre-*Dark Side* days.

With the debut performance sold out and three more shows at the Half Moon in Putney also successful, the quintet undertook a European tour in autumn, following it up with an American tour in 2019. One of the most unexpected aspects of this latter tour was an appearance by Roger Waters at the New York date, where, to the delight of the audience, he sang with the band for *Set The Controls For The Heart Of The Sun.*

For all the bitterness and strife in Pink Floyd, Mason has long emphasised that Waters is his friend. The pair were together as musical partners from the earliest times of the group. That Waters made an appearance to sing one of his most admired songs speaks not just of Mason's ambition for his group, but also of the respect given to one of Waters' best songs, both by him and by the group's legions of fans.

After Covid-19, two further tours were arranged, both of them successful. Recorded material also became available on CD and vinyl: the live double CD and DVD film *Live At The Roundhouse*, live renditions of *See Emily Play* and *Vegetable Man* for Record Store Day in 2020, and a live version of *Echoes* for RSD 2025. These choices are significant. *Echoes* will always remain one of the most beloved Pink Floyd songs, and Mason was at the heart of its creation when the original was recorded. Choosing that song cannot have been difficult. The choice of *See Emily Play* is interesting because that song was a single release before *The Piper At The Gates Of Dawn*, and not on the album. These days, though its charm remains undiminished (YouTube videos of the group performing it on 6 July 1967, introduced by Alan "Fluff" Freeman for the BBC's Top Of The Pops, have millions of combined views) it is not as well-known as the 1970s material. But that is not surprising. As I write this, 1967 is two generations in the past, and that is grandfather territory. But the choice of *Vegetable Man* is at least as significant. This is a Syd Barrett song that was considered as a possible 45 release or for inclusion on *A Saucerful Of Secrets* – a song which could be a twin of his *Jugband Blues*. But the darkness of the lyrics, Barrett's mental state and the quality of the group's other music meant that it was left out. The 2018 live version was its first modern appearance.

It is Nick Mason who has kept the extraordinary legacy of the early Pink Floyd in the limelight. Those first six years of the group's life following their signing to EMI are today just as influential as the 1970s work. Some have argued that the use of instrumental and psychedelic techniques – these days, space rock is a huge sub-genre – is largely down to the influence of the group, while Barrett himself remains one of the most influential songwriters in pop and rock music history. It is the heartbeat of the group, Nick Mason, who is responsible these days for taking the early music to audiences new and old.

Chapter 20

Looking Back

So… what did it all amount to? Looking back from 2026 across six decades… what did it mean?

When I came back home from university in the early 1980s for out-of-term holidays, my father and I would have what became known in our family as "the music argument." Actually, it was not really much of an argument, more a statement of our respective positions. He, a classical music snob and wannabe jazzer, thought that rock and pop music, such as his son was now obsessed with, could not be compared with Bach and Beethoven. He conceived of a definite and obvious line between the two forms, with classical music being infinitely superior to noisy rock music. That was his comparison. I was a little more relaxed. Even in those days, naive about culture and desperate to escape my family (they were in Shropshire, I was in London), I recognised that my father was a superb pianist. But I did not appreciate then the cultural background from which he came. It was all culture to me, of various sorts, with classical music in my mind an equivalent to history. So my side of the discussion was that the two forms of music could be compared, and indeed should be, because that was an interesting path to follow. I gave rock music a significance and gravity which my father thought imbecilic. In his eyes, I was just his son, getting involved in music that had no depth and would not last. Yet even then, struggling to articulate my feelings about the music I loved, I was aware that the truly great groups – Tangerine Dream, Yes, The Beatles, and of course Pink Floyd – would last. Their music would live on. I sensed it without knowing why that would be the case. Later on, my father came to grasp the importance of The Beatles, but he never understood Tangerine Dream or Yes. He and I agreed on Steve Reich, but Yes and Genesis… according to him, they were destined for music's rubbish bin.

Rock music is Art. I am happy to use a capital A there. Ever since 1967, when The Beatles gave the world *Sgt. Pepper's Lonely Hearts Club Band,* rock and, to a lesser extent, pop music have been able to stretch out and explore territory that before did not exist. For all the reverence proffered to that extraordinary album *Revolver,* it was *Sgt Pepper* that changed the world. That trailblazing forty minutes showed what could be done in a recording studio, with drums, bass, guitars and keyboards, and maybe an orchestra and a swarmandal. It catapulted a formerly quite limited cultural music format, albeit one that was in a process of sophistication, into something entirely new, something that stood with confidence in its new landscape by itself, on its own two feet, inviting us to take it seriously because of the sheer brilliance of the vision.

How did we know it was brilliant? Because our emotions to us so. Impossible to listen to *With A Little Help From My Friends* and *She's Leaving Home* without feeling sad or melancholic. Impossible to hear *Being For The Benefit Of Mr Kite!* without a wry grin at its effusive wit. Impossible to listen to *Within You Without You* without feeling wonder at that combination of Indian and Western instruments. *When I'm 64...* McCartney wrote that when he was fourteen. Awesome.

From 1967 onwards, although pop music continued along its commercial trajectory, there was an option to do something different. Bands could head off into rock territory based more or less on the American blues tradition, or they could make statements of high art. That was possible after The Beatles. They forged the template. They allowed their album to be a touchstone for so much outside music: social and cultural issues, youth politics and the arrival of a new, colourful generation. Drugs, of course. Permissiveness and conservatism, which, by accident or otherwise, are now manifested by our thoughts on LSD and our thoughts on the throwback Edwardian veneer used by the Fab 4 in order to become "characters" that they could inhabit. Two years later, those characters would come to life again in one of the greatest animations ever made, *Yellow Submarine,* which at once expanded the mind and assumed the Edwardian clothes and style worn by the LP's concept. For *Sgt Pepper* was a concept album. It had a framework, a purpose and a meaning outside of music. Some, later on, would find that pretentious.

Others, a group in which I include myself, found and still find it very useful when making or listening to music.

I suspect that most of the albums I have made with my group or as a solo artist are concept albums, by which I mean that they have a concept, whether or not that concept is immediately obvious. I find such templates invaluable when preparing music. So, when progressive rock began to emerge from the too-whimsical, too-airy fairy psychedelic scene, it was the concept album that, for many groups, became a useful format. For Pink Floyd that was as true as for The Beatles in 1967 or King Crimson in 1969.

Even *The Piper At The Gates Of Dawn* – never recorded as a concept album, and little influenced by *Sgt Pepper*, even though the group were working insidethe same recording studio as The Beatles – had a concept through which it could be assimilated and understood. That concept was one emerging from Syd Barrett's mind: his love of childhood motifs, his joy at the books of his favourite authors, but also the more adult world of psychedelia and permissiveness around LSD. I would say the debut Pink Floyd album was a concept album for that reason, even though it is never presented so and was never conceived along those lines. It does have a purpose, an intensity of meaning founded in Barrett's mental world, that transcends "mere" pop or rock music. It is relevant and loved today for that reason, in ways the follow-up LP, musically as superb, is not. That such significance is given to the debut is down to Barrett, his songwriting and his concepts, whether they are implicit or not.

Barrett was a natural, like McCartney. He could not write songs in any way other than his own. He was a one-off. The concept of *The Piper At The Gates Of Dawn* was implicit, revealed to the listener through Barrett's use of melody and the style and concerns of his lyrics. But as a natural, he was sincere. He was genuine. Nick Mason recalls being surprised at Barrett's social ease, approaching Mason and introducing himself, something English chaps rarely did. Barrett radiated charisma. Concept albums where they seem pretentious are insincere, the concept used as braggadocio, as style over substance, as a gravity that is not present in the music. Such albums have no charisma. None of those criticisms can be applied to any Pink Floyd album.

As the group began to reorganise itself and seek new horizons in the post-Barrett downturn and malaise of the late 1960s, the blissful dreams of the Summer of Love already turning into nightmares, Roger Waters emerged as a songwriter of significance. Even in 1967 he had mocked British social traditions, his debut song *Take Up Thy Stethoscope And Walk* critical of how the medical profession can treat individuals as objects, not people. Although many of his late 1960s songs were more pastoral and easy going, by the time it came to *Echoes* on *Meddle,* and to *The Dark Side Of The Moon, Wish You Were Here* and *Animals,* he achieved a level of social comment that made him a brilliant observer and analyst of how individual human beings were damaged by contemporary society, how they coped with the conditions they found themselves in, and how they behaved as a consequence. Waters' concepts and lyrics, allied with the group's exceptional music, became a mirror to the feelings of the fans.

This ability of some rock music groups to manifest, reflect and interpret the feelings of their fans made them a vital part of growing up in the 1970s. Most of these fans were male, and were, as a consequence, not so adept as women at conveying their own feelings, and perhaps not so keen to show their true emotions. All that, in traditional, patriarchal Britain in the 1970s, was something for girls. And few progressive groups were interested in down-to-earth, modern social issues. Genesis was one, especially with Peter Gabriel as their frontman. Pink Floyd was another. That relationship between the music and lyrics of the group and the lives of their fans became another reason for the increase of their fanbase as their concepts turned to the human condition and the travails of modern society. Pink Floyd began to reflect in a way that was much more significant than usual how the modern young individual was feeling. The feelings inspired by their music became something worth expressing. If Roger Waters was writing about empathy, that meant it was significant. A fan may have realised that before, of course, and had perhaps even acted on their own feelings, but somehow having it presented in a cultural, immersive, understandable form made it easier to assimilate and grasp. That music itself is about the human emotional experience – about what is most valuable to us, most significant – added to the impact.

The themes dealt with by Waters at the height of his songwriting with Pink Floyd were deep and intense. It was human stuff that really mattered. Because the group were themselves exploring this territory, because they were sincere, and because they were lucky enough to be perceived as part of a burgeoning cultural trend, they achieved an impact most groups could only dream of. Yet they were set apart from that trend also: they were different. That doubled their impact. Many of their themes were aspects of the connections between people, and what happens when such a connection is thwarted by social conditions. Waters was a perceptive and able interpreter of such lives, representing through music the mental damage and pain inflicted by what he saw around him: by capitalist society, conservative society, warlike society, disconnected society. He saw the bleak heart of capitalism, the thick hide of tradition, the ruination and madness of war, the lonely crowd. All this was presented to fans in a way that made their own realities somewhat more real. If they felt disconnected from others, they did at least feel connected to the band's music – to the idea of Pink Floyd.

The music I grew up with and came to love between the ages of fifteen and twenty-five has left an indelible mark on my mind. I think that is the way with most music-lovers navigating that part of their lives. I would wager that a significant proportion of Floyd fans could lie back, turn down the lights and play in the privacy of their mind the entirety of *The Dark Side Of The Moon*, feeling all the same feelings as if it were the LP in 1973. We never forget the music we love at that age because it becomes part of our identity. That means, when we ask the question *Why?* of ourselves – the *Who?* question – the answer can be expressed in terms of *The Dark Side Of The Moon*. The album therefore, becomes an external aspect of our identity, which, joy of joys, we know we share with others. All this is a quintessential human experience.

In the 1970s, that experience of sharing important LPs by significant artists with like-minded individuals was also mediated by LP covers. For all young people passing through the formative years of their adult lives in and around that decade, music became a vital part of declaring yourself and finding your kindred. There were many such clubs, each symbolised by an ur-band: the Floyd, Zep, Yes, the Tangs. I remember bumping into a French fan of Klaus Schulze in London's Virgin Megastore in the early 1980s as I was browsing the Schulze LP rack. I can recall to this day the excitement on his face when he realised we both 'got' the great KS. He told me in broken English how he had attended a Schulze concert during the 1970s, "which was a dream, you know?" Music lovers never forget. How could we?

Such experiences are our mental fabric. They literally sustain us, as well as manifesting our characters in society.

It so happened that Pink Floyd was one of the most significant of ur-bands exactly at the time when this LP effect was most prevalent: 1967 to the beginning of the 1980s. Their main musical trajectory matched that period. It was therefore a matter of importance that their LP covers were iconic and immediately recognisable. This social signalling could be done with the ear, the prism, the burning man or the flying pig. In Exeter's HMV store at the moment, there are a number of silhouettes painted on the rear stairs, one of which is a burning man. It is immediately clear what that refers to. That image is a succinct representation of something profound and complex. It is itself an icon. I took a selfie there, of course.

Certain rock bands become exemplars, too. In some cases, that means they and their members are idolised, or, if not idolised, then appreciated to a degree which, from the outside, looks a bit weird. That is the bleaker side of being a cultural exemplar. But some bands manage to dramatise important human experiences to an extent which makes them susceptible to being held up as an exemplar instead of being idolised. Many bands have both: the wide-eyed fans and the chin-stroking appreciators. I suppose I belong in the latter category. I don't want to be Syd Barrett, Roger Waters, David Gilmour, Richard Wright or Nick Mason. I do have a bit of a beard to play with.

Some people do want to be their idols, however. Some people find it difficult to assemble a character amidst the flak and obstacles of life, the torments, the bad luck, the quiet desperation which is the English way. Some people want to be Klaus Schulze and create music just like his. Some people want to be John McLaughlin, playing exceedingly fast. Some people wish they were Jimmy Page.

Idolisation is a dangerous path. If you cannot be yourself and so have to be somebody else, you open yourself up to great disappointment, disillusionment and anger when your idol, like all idols, turns out to be human. Then there is the unrealistic assessment of your idol and their world. Much of that is fantasy, which, for all its balms, is not usually a great place to make a home. "Know thyself", runs the maxim carved in stone at the Temple of Apollo in Delphi. Lack of self-knowledge can be soothed by coming to know somebody else, be that Pink or Pink Floyd, but it is a perilous route to take because it is, by definition, inauthentic. It was precisely those inauthentic human experiences that Roger Waters was writing about in *Animals* and *The Wall*. You become a Dog at your peril, because dogs get drowned once they have served their utilitarian purpose. You become a Pig at your peril in a world where competition is ruthless and nobody can reveal the truth of themself. And it is best not to be a Sheep. One of the most cutting of modern insults is *sheeple,* yet how many Pink Floyd fans in modern online groups endlessly telling themselves that Pink Floyd Are The Best Band Ever would see themselves as sheeple? Few, I suspect.

It was that great Welsh rock band Manic Street Preachers who best broached the matter of their fans. In their iconic post-Richey Edwards song *A Design For Life,* Nicky Wire both set out the critical importance of knowing yourself through education, through the power of libraries and the importance of work, whilst at the same time depicting his audience as unable to speak about love and only interested in getting drunk.

It is surely only a coincidence that Pink Floyd's *Sheep* was gestated around the same time John Lydon lambasted his audience on Tony Wilson's *So It Goes* television show thusly: *Get off your arses!* There was something new emerging in Britain, something frightening but authentic, dangerous yet true to a human ideal that had been repressed for years. Roger Waters could have been waiting for it. John Lydon exploited it with all the shocking brilliance of his wounded character. Pink Floyd and Sex Pistols were both exemplars. They both spoke with authenticity, albeit in musical genres opposed to one another.

Pink Floyd, in their early days, were exemplars of the idea of hippie freedom, of what then was called the permissive society, of freedom, of liberty, of Liberty Caps and acid. Their existence was at once a consequence of social change and an example of it, manifesting new core beliefs in a rapidly changing world. Syd Barrett especially epitomised a set of desires and ethics that The Man – the bloated dead weight of British tradition and conservatism – sought to repress. The police were the pigs. Yet in their post-Barrett incarnation, through the wit and insight of Roger Waters and his concepts and lyrics, the group became exemplars of a yearning to be more true to deeper human ideals: to authenticity, to emotional truth, to community, connection, union. Those Floyd fans who had insight into themselves, who had grasped the maxim "Know thyself," were those who responded to the group as exemplars. They may have been classic examples of English emotional constipation, but at least through the music they loved, they had a chance of deeper self-knowledge, which, if they were lucky, would allow them a chance of a happier, more meaningful life.

To paraphrase Bob Dylan, the highest purpose of Art is to inspire. Through the first half of the 1970s and into the period which begat *Animals* and *The Wall*, Pink Floyd were in that most lucky of positions from which they could make the great music they wished to, convey the thoughts and concepts they wished to, point out what the obstacles were, and perhaps even offer a way out of the dilemma. This was done through songs and albums which we now regard as iconic. That status comes from the authenticity of the vision as well as the luck involved with being alive and musically active at just the right point in history.

Creativity is a slippery concept. It is often characterised as a thing in itself, or a way of feeling and thinking, or a connection to some ethereal source of inspiration which flows through the creator, or some kind of inbuilt, perhaps even genetic ability that comes from having a particular sort of mind and a particular sort of brain.

That latter notion is closest to the truth. Creativity, though, is not a thing. It is instead a response to a thing, where the thing being responded to is reality. Creativity is the private response to the experience of reality as constructed in the mind of a human individual. That is why all creative expression – all Art, as it manifests in society – is interpretation. That being the case, it comes to certain types of individuals to be the most creative.

It was the brilliant psychotherapist Dorothy Rowe who explained that people either experience their inner reality as more real and coherent than the outside world – what we these days might call introverts – or experience the outside world as more real than their inner landscape – what we might call extroverts. Later thinkers made distinctions between sensitive introverts, the quiet ones, and others, more gregarious, particularly in cultures like America, which prioritises extroversion above all else and which more often than not considers introversion a form of mental difficulty to be overcome. This was the gist of Susan Cain's groundbreaking book *Quiet,* which linked introversion and love of music in ways not previously explored in depth.

This is not to say that the five members of Pink Floyd were necessarily all introverts. Yet that quietness, that reflectivity, that sensitivity to music in all its forms, that urge to create, that love of depth, that desire to connect through profound thinking are all hallmarks of the introvert way. Each of the members of the group blends introversion with extroversion in their own way. David Gilmour, for instance, explains that the guitar is the best instrument for him to express his feelings. That is a classic statement for an introvert, for a quiet man of depth.

Great art inspires, dramatises or conveys what it is like to interpret the world, connects individuals and, having connected, offers shared ownership. All of us Floyd fans experience union through that group's musical culture. We are all fellow travellers on the Pink Floyd road. When our feelings match those evoked by Gilmour's expressive, profound guitar playing, we are in union with others who feel the same. But, just as importantly, we are in union with ourselves. We are being true to our own characters. Great music has the power to make this happen because it appeals to all that is valuable to us, which happens in the main through our emotions. When that perception of human value is the same as that experienced by somebody else, a union of interpretation of the world is forged, something all human beings long for, whether they know it or not. This is why two people who love *The Dark Side Of The Moon* can share an unspoken communication. It is why the smile on the face of the French Klaus Schulze fan whom I bumped into at the Virgin Megastore was an immediate signal of the deep connection we shared. That was a marvellous moment, significant to me, which is why I have never forgotten it. I wonder if he recalls it?

Having shared great art, there follows the issue of what then happens to it. Although the four members of the group, upon hearing the mix of *The Dark Side Of The Moon* in their mixing booth for the first time, realised that they had created something special, they had no idea that, for reasons described above, but also because of accidents of music history, they were about to release an album which would go on to be the fourth bestselling album of all time. They could not know that they had created an object of reverence, iconic and recognised across the world. Yet that is what happened.

An icon is a representative image, object or person. An icon is always symbolic of something profound. Such are the albums *The Dark Side Of*

The Moon and *Wish You Were Here*. Yet the journey of those albums was one from private to public ownership. Even within the group, there was a motion from private, personal ownership, that of Waters and his lyrics and concept, to one shared by his fellow musicians in the group and the company of technicians supporting them.

Yet the journey from group ownership to that by hundreds of millions of people worldwide was the more extraordinary one, a journey that transformed the albums in question. In effect, the group lost *The Dark Side Of The Moon*. Instead, they became fellow travellers alongside it. A strange thing happens to creative people when their work moves from private ownership to large-scale public ownership, which is that they must acclimatise to the feelings and opinions of millions of others: fans especially, but also reviewers and other commentators. That a piece of art takes on a life of its own is a weird experience. In some respects, it is a little like the move of a child into adulthood: leaving home, becoming independent. Although that child is always the parents' own, it is never the same. The child becomes part of the wider society. This is what happened to those two iconic Pink Floyd albums.

Some artists do not like this process and become defensive about their precious work. Some authors do not like changes to their novels, made, for instance, by directors when those works are filmed. But they have to get used to public ownership. The four men of Pink Floyd had to get used to being fellow travellers alongside *The Dark Side Of The Moon*. For instance, they had to get used to the idea of an album called *Dub Side Of The Moon*.

There can be feelings of frustration, not least when an artist believes their work has been misinterpreted or misrepresented. Roger Waters, for instance, gets annoyed when people claim Syd Barrett invented space rock. Being misunderstood is particularly uncomfortable for a lot of creative people because one of the main reasons for making art is to communicate an inner world; a viewpoint, a state of being. When that inner world is misunderstood, especially if it is misrepresented in public discourse, that is a horrible experience. Alas, those who create iconic albums have to face such issues.

Feelings of confusion also arise when fans' favourites are not the artist's own. Although the proportion of Floyd fans who do not like *Wish You Were Here* must be minuscule, if it even exists at all, those (like me) who adore the

Atom Heart Mother Suite, which both Waters and Gilmour have dismissed in various interviews, must be something of an oddity to those who wrote and recorded the music. But we musicians must all look back on our catalogues with grace and flexibility, because that body of work is in effect no longer our own. Fans are well within their rights to love work we ourselves do not.

Another significant feature of Pink Floyd, especially through the first half of the 1970s, was that they illustrated a rock music truism. Sometimes, a group is more than the sum of its parts. When that happens, their music, their status and their perceived value changes.

It is notable amongst fans of the ultimate free festival psychedelic group Ozric Tentacles that almost every fan who has stuck by them through thick and thin since the original members met around a campfire at the 1983 Stonehenge Free Festival loves the earlier band format above all others. During the last two decades, a more streamlined band has been recording albums, although live, there is usually a bassist and a drummer. But so many fans, when they talk about more recent albums, bemoan the use of bass synths and drum software, and yearn for the good old days when Roly Wynne was on bass and Merv Pepler was their drummer. Or, in fact, for any five-man version of the group.

There is a reason for this kind of nostalgia, one that applies to Pink Floyd. When a group becomes more than the sum of its parts, a special kind of union emerges around them, one which all human beings desire. We act so often to overcome that sense of apartness created by the fact that we all live in the world of our subjective feelings – conscious, yes, our feelings and thoughts communicable, but separated nevertheless. To see such apartness being overcome in a transcendent display of union, especially through an emotionally positive experience like music, is one of the great experiences of life. Music lovers desire this as much as anyone else, but they have their own channel through which such a union can be experienced. It is a feeling like no other.

Most musicians speak of the special occasions in their life when intuition, subliminal communication and shared goals create this "greater than the sum of the parts" experience. The members of Led Zeppelin, for example, all felt it when they began working together. But this is how all good music works. It is best followed, not controlled. It is best experienced, not planned. Even when recording an album, these special occasions crop up – it does not have to be during joint music-making. To see it live is another peak experience.

For Pink Floyd, the studio side of *Ummagumma* was the album that showed they were precisely the sum of their parts. *The Dark Side Of The Moon* and *Wish You Were Here* showed they were more.

Surely the most memorable aspect of Pink Floyd's legacy is their songs, which sounds like this author stating the obvious, but I mean in a particular way. I mean the *melodies* of those songs.

Pink Floyd were active at a time when melody was either a natural part of songwriting or something that was prioritised. About twenty years ago, I began thinking about melody in my own music. I am uncertain what the motivation was for this – perhaps a personal need to return to a time in pop history when songs seemed more tuneful. At the time, my band was active, so it seemed natural for me to understand melody by trying to write it. Of course, that was not easy at first. In the end, I found that what worked for me was what I call the Neil Young Method. Young goes with what comes to him first thing in the morning, when his subconscious dreaming mind is close to his conscious mind. In such a way, he wrote gorgeous songs with beautiful melodies, like *After The Gold Rush, Only Love Can Break Your Heart* and *Heart Of Gold*.

Whether I found myself able to write a unique melody is a question best left to those who remember my band and bought the albums. What I can say is that using Young's method, I found many melodies that seemed fresh and original to me, and after a while, I had more than I needed.

Twenty years on, I often find myself considering what seems to me to be the diminishing importance of melody in modern pop and rock music. I feel this is symptomatic of some deeper malaise. It has struck me during the last couple of decades that more popular music now than that of, say, the 1960s or 1970s, is lacking those wonderful, sometimes extraordinary melodies: I'm thinking of Paul McCartney's classics, many Motown classics, The Byrds, the Beach Boys, John Phillips' songs, Paul Simon, Donald Fagen of Steely Dan, and so on. Did something happen around the turn of the millennium that sucked some of the melody out of popular music in the West?

It seems to me now that such a thing might have happened. As a practising musician, I now wonder if it had something to do with the increasing use of computers in the recording studio. Using software rather than analogue tape can channel musicians in a certain direction: loop-based music using samples, for instance. Some groups can use loops and samples in an original way, but for me, something is lost around this particular time. But perhaps there is more to it than computer software.

What *is* melody? Melody for me is a direct connection to the emotional heart of human existence. With melody, feelings can be evoked without the need for words – you only have to think of instrumental themes like Tchaikovsky's *Piano Concerto No. 1,* or many themes from famous films, like Francis Lai's unforgettable theme from *Love Story.* Melody is our path into deep feeling, emotion and mood – think of the theme from *The Snowman…*

So I can't help wondering if the loss of melody from popular music is diagnostic of a more profound problem. We live in a world where computers *are* the environment, not just some handy device *in* the environment. Our world has become one of calculation, algorithm, statistics. The analogue age is over: this is the digital age. Could it be that the loss of melody in pop and rock music is a symptom of emotion, and therefore of human values, receding from our world? Could the reported increase in ennui, in numbness, in the Western world also be symptomatic of such a lack?

Perhaps this observation explains why the so-called legacy acts – artists, bands, and groups from the previous century – are enjoying renewed popularity. Perhaps the much-reduced melodic power of so much modern music is the reason listeners are turning to Pink Floyd, amongst many others, those groups from parents' and grandparents' times who knew how to write a melody and recognised the critical importance of it to their songs. Perhaps this is why, in recent times, the notion of "songwriting" has become synonymous with "lyric writing." I do not think writing lyrics is the same as writing a song. If you write lyrics, you are a poet. If you set your lyrics to a speaking voice or a tuneless melody – what musicologists call a horizontal melody – you have not written a song. A song *must* have melody and lyrics. It can have a horizontal melody over a good chord sequence, but it could have a vertical melody. Syd Barrett knew how to write a unique vertical melody, as did the others in Pink Floyd. A large part of the immense power of *The Dark Side Of The Moon* is in those unforgettable melodies.

As mentioned above, the loss of melody from popular music may be the sonic equivalent of a canary in a mine. It is telling us that something bad is happening, something that too many people either do not realise is happening or cannot explain. Our world is losing part of its humanity.

One final aspect of the legacy of Pink Floyd lies in their mystique. I cannot be the only uneasy observer of the fragmentation of classic rock albums into lengthy, separate parts, to be marketed and resold to punters who already have the albums in question. And not just because of the obvious commercial impulse to make more money from something that already exists and which needs no cash input, but because that act to me destroys the *mystique* of the album.

The Immersion Editions of *The Dark Side Of The Moon* and *Wish You Were Here* contain alternate, unreleased mixes, in the former case that made in 1972 by Alan Parsons. To me, that deed removes the mystique from the album and, in doing so, diminishes it. To put it in terms of another masterpiece, it was J.R.R. Tolkien's Gandalf the Grey who said: *He who breaks a thing to find out what it is has left the path of wisdom.*

Mystique and Pink Floyd's place in the national psyche led to their music appearing in the 2012 London Olympic Games opening ceremony – a video clip early in the event. The flying pig from the LP cover of *Animals* was tethered to Battersea Power Station while a helicopter flew past. Soon after this, the chimes from *Time* sounded out as the helicopter flew over the Houses of Parliament. *Eclipse*, meanwhile, played during the firework display after the Olympic flame was lit. And another icon joined Pink Floyd: Mike Oldfield, *Tubular Bells*.

Mystique, enigma and mystery are part of the joy of experiencing music. I would choose listening to the original album for the experience alone every time, over having it explained to me in detail and at considerable expense. Personally, I do think those Immersion Editions are a cash cow, but, more importantly, they transform what was previously a magical experience into an explicable one.

The magic of Pink Floyd does not diminish with age. A young, modern generation is finding that out. This is a hopeful sign.

Chapter 21

There Is No Dark Side Of The Moon… Matter Of Fact, It's All Dark

On the fiftieth anniversary of the release of *The Dark Side Of The Moon*, Roger Waters put out his *Redux* version that he had recorded with some session musicians. He attached himself once again to that album name and that group name.

But what if they had been Anderson Council? Would they have been as successful?

Pink Floyd is a name comprising a pair of one syllable words, a name that trips off the tongue easily. Anderson Council is a bit of a mouthful, missing the colour reference used by a lot of bands of this era, yet too short to be one of those extended names beloved of psychedelic art musicians, especially in America. Pink Floyd it was.

Can we from our sixty-year perspective perform the necessary thought experiment to undo all that Floydian pinkness? It is difficult. Pink Floyd, like Mike Oldfield and The Beatles, are part of the nation's fabric now. History has given them a place offered to very few. They *are* us, representing us even if we do not like the music. But then again… who doesn't like The Beatles, Oldfield and Pink Floyd? You would have to be a particularly grumpy individual to diss that trio of musical brilliance. It would almost be un-British to try.

Pink Floyd have transcended mere fame, fortune and extended public life to achieve symbolic significance. They actually represent something British through their music, their LP covers, and the intertwining of their lives with our own. We cannot convert them into Anderson Council.

Pink Floyd are our national character, our emotional reserve also, our ambition, our creativity, our very imaginations. Their music lives in our shared memory through a process of symbiosis. What was done cannot be undone. But nobody would want to anyway.

My Pink Floyd Top 20

1. Echoes

The beginning of the greatness – music of sublime beauty but also strangeness, whose crows, choir and melodies combine to create twenty-three minutes of perfection. For me, this was the moment the group changed from four marvellous musicians to a marvellous group, whose whole, as is recognised by millions of fans worldwide, is greater than the sum of its parts.

2. Us And Them

Surely one of the most wonderful songs about the dark side of the human condition – and one of the most moving songs the group ever recorded, which for me always raised the hairs on the back of my neck in recognition of quite how sharp the barbs of this song are.

3. Chapter 24

I think this could be Syd Barrett's most remarkable melody. From somebody whose intuitive facility for melody was so great, it seems almost too simple, like a childhood lullaby; yet its depth and power remain undimmed after half a century. That's the mark of genius.

4. A Saucerful Of Secrets

The greatest of the group's early psychedelic, spacey long-form works, whose ability to evoke strange places, far horizons and depths to profound to plumb make it the beginning of so much in the same vein that followed. The haunting choral section at the end makes it beautiful too.

5. Julia Dream

Alas, Richard Wright remains under-appreciated as a songwriter. But he truly was great. This gorgeous song reminds all true Floyd fans of the depth and power of his musical vision, which, following the departure of Barrett, was one of the foundations upon which they rebuilt themselves.

6. Cirrus Minor

Quite the most beautiful evocation of Englishness you could wish to hear – lazy, strange, sunny, and recorded with a brilliant use of natural sounds. This song stands at the head of a long line of such songs that during the end of the 1960s the group wrote and recorded; and those birds singing remain as fixed and vivid in my memory as does Gilmour's plangent voice.

7. Any Colour You Like

The freewheeling, rapturous, cosmic and mesmeric instrumental twin of *Us And Them*, whose keyboards and synthesisers combine to create one of the group's most sumptuous musical works. It is the delay on that lead synthesiser which makes this song, extending Wright's playing into a hypnotic space all his own.

8. Breathe

One of very few songs that as a tyro guitarist I learned to play. The relaxed tempo, spacious sound and intense lyrics make this one of the group's masterpieces, the first of a handful on their iconic 1973 album.

9. Shine On You Crazy Diamond

Somehow nostalgic and realistic simultaneously, this timeless work, when gathered together from its various parts, stands as a memorial both to Barrett the man and to his legacy. In nostalgia, it describes pain: in realism it paints a vivid portrait, with four men standing behind the enigmatic silhouette of a silent Syd.

10. Atom Heart Mother

For all that Waters and Gilmour downplay the value of this epic psychedelic suite, its glorious ambition, melodies and inspired musicianship combine to create in my mind something not far off a masterpiece – and I never get bored of hearing it.

11. *Wish You Were Here*
One of the group's most beautiful songs, and with one of Waters' most profound lyrics, this piece stands as the group's enduring message to the power of human connection. In just a handful of words they say everything the listener needs to know about the reasons we should embrace one another: actuality, legacy and history.

12. *Green Is The Colour*
Always a favourite song for me because of its gorgeous tune and that evocation – which Floyd did so well as they found their feet in the post-Barrett world – of sunlight in summer. It's pastoral and natural all at the same time.

13. *See-saw*
Another of Wright's best songs, one in which the skill of the recording and the inspired playing make a piece that far outweighs its apparently simple structure. At once melodious, mysterious and haunting, it encapsulates everything that Wright gave to the band in 1968.

14. *Dogs*
Of their later works, this has to be one of the best – lyrically and musically. Yet it's the appearance of novel technology and new recording techniques, especially in the spooky vocoder/delay section, that for me raises this work from good to great. It also shows how brilliant Waters could be when he worked for the good of the group as a whole.

15. *On The Turning Away*
My favourite of the Gilmour-era songs, I think the melody of this one is akin to Paul McCartney's greatest. It has that timeless feel of songs which sound like ancient folk melodies, but which are in fact quite new. A work too of great lyrical perception.

16. *Fat Old Sun*
I love this for its languid, sun-soaked simplicity, from an era when the group were creating a good few songs in this arena. This one too shows how much Gilmour the great guitarist absorbed from the blues tradition, which was to make the *feel* of his playing unique.

17. *The Gnome*

So quirky a song probably wouldn't make any other top 20 lists, but this one has always been a favourite of mine. It matches the eccentric imagination of Barrett with his melodic genius, at once ever so English and yet universal, like childhood itself. Side 2 of *The Piper At The Gates Of Dawn* is unmatched when it comes to unique, never-to-be-repeated sonic vision.

18. *A Pillow Of Winds*

Another of the group's sunny masterpieces, this one marries updated 1970s production techniques with one of Gilmour's best singing performances. It drifts and idles by, light as gossamer, glinting in golden sunbeams.

19. *Grantchester Meadows*

Grantchester lies within the orbit of those Cambridge landscapes which informed a lot of the group's early experiences in music. The naturalistic lyrics of this Waters composition are particularly evocative. It's always been a favourite song of mine from their exceptional catalogue.

20. *The Scarecrow*

Ah, Syd – you master of melody! Only you could come up with so extraordinary a tune and place lyrics so eccentrically English over the top. Nobody else could have written this one.

Charts of favourite songs from a group or sub-genre are perhaps a bit of a cliche, but in their defence they are great fun and they can have the effect of focusing thought on the creative output of classic groups. When Bluesky regular James Tansley instituted a Pink Floyd Top 20 in spring 2025, the results, voted upon by various of his followers and promoted on the #PinkFloydTop20 hashtag, were fascinating.

Top of the thirty most popular tracks in terms of votes was a song that never even made it to my top 20, though I recognise its majestic qualities. *Comfortably Numb* was that song, and no doubt its pole position was as much to do with Gilmour's transcendent guitar solos as with the melody or the lyrics. It is without doubt one of a couple of solid gold classics from *The Wall*.

Second was a true icon of Floyd songwriting: *Wish You Were Here*. This song touches the hearts of innumerable people, through the sincerity of its lyrics, its warmth and generosity, and of course for that unique vocal delivery courtesy David Gilmour. It can be compared with classic Beatles songs which, through their extraordinary and continuing influence, have become classics in the same way that certain traditional folk standards have. Such songs inhabit a cultural space which speaks of true Englishness, which we can all hold close, and which we all understand the value of. *Wish You Were Here* is equivalent to *Yesterday*, or *All You Need Is Love*, which Elvis Costello in 1985 at Live Aid memorably introduced as "this old northern English folk song." *Wish You Were Here* says something about our musical and social culture which cannot be eroded by the passage of time.

Third on the Bluesky list was *Shine On You Crazy Diamond (1-5)*, the value of which cannot be disputed. Coming from that second iconic album of the group's 1970s run, its place in the affections of Floyd fans – and perhaps even amongst the nation at large – is immovable. Fourth on the list was top of my list: *Echoes*. Again, this epic song looms so large in the canon of both group and progressive rock as a whole it can never be demoted far down the list. *Time* and *Us And Them* were fifth and sixth, with *Dogs* number seven – all expected chart positions.

Number eight was *High Hopes* from *The Division Bell*. This song also looms large in the thoughts of Pink Floyd fans, but perhaps for different reasons than for those above. Lyrically, it was not a million miles away from the sentiments of *Shine On You Crazy Diamond* – an evocation of the local and personal origins of the remarkable men who comprised the group. *High Hopes* was all about reflecting on the passing of time and the consequences of ambition. Wrapped in images of Cambridge and the Syd Barrett era of the group, its lyrics were the song's heart rather than the music. Written by Gilmour and his then-girlfriend Polly Samson, the sincerity, the mixture of nostalgia and delight at ambitions achieved, and the emotional generosity of the song all contributed to its high placement in the Bluesky top 20. It was also a courageous song, in that it accepted that creative ambition, like life itself, is limited by time. In that regard it was akin to David Bowie's song *Lazarus,* the video of which showed him entering a cupboard, the doors of which he then closed: death itself. *High Hopes* was a song that celebrated good luck but was unafraid of acknowledging success, for this song was no boast. That Gilmour himself recognised the immense value of what he had achieved, and was wise enough to write *High Hopes* about all that at a time when he thought Pink Floyd was over forever, is a testament to his great worth as a musician and as a man.

Two more cuts from *The Wall* made the next two places: *Hey You* and *Another Brick In The Wall*. Both of these songs are melodically sophisticated, memorable for sure, and that no doubt accounted for their popularity. The latter of the two songs was a worldwide hit, that with its unforgettable video featuring the art of Gerald Scarfe, burned itself into the memories of all watching at the time.

Further tracks from *Meddle, The Dark Side Of The Moon, Wish You Were Here* and *Animals* occupied the next lot of spaces up to number 18, with the first "early" track coming in comparatively low – at least, in my view. But *Set The Controls For The Heart Of The Sun* was always a fan favourite, as was *Astronomy Domine* coming in at 20.

Sorrow came next, with *See Emily Play* and *Interstellar Overdrive* following on the list – more fan favourites from the Barrett era. *Fearless* and *Fat Old Sun* took the next places, with *Run Like Hell* at 27 – a not unexpected accolade for that track. *In The Flesh?* was for me a bizarre appearance, with *Mother* and *Have A Cigar* next up to complete the top thirty.

To my mind, this list missed something of what I find most valuable about Pink Floyd, which is their exploration of psychedelic and progressive rock music in the context of melody in particular. For me, that *Mother, Have A Cigar* and *Run Like Hell* got mentions at the bottom of the charts instead of *Chapter 24, The Gnome* and *Scarecrow* – which eclipse that trio of voted songs as the Beatles eclipse Oasis – amounted to something of a missed opportunity. The Rick Wright songs which appear in my top 20 were also missed by the Bluesky list, which I find a little disappointing, although his presence is very much remembered in all the *Wish You Were Here* songs. Then again, it could be that the 1970s catalogue of songs carries such significance compared with the (perhaps less well known) 1960s songs their value is heightened by that effect, leading to high placements.

As I said above, these games of song ranking are in essence a bit of fun, intended to celebrate and reflect upon beloved music. Yet they do focus the mind on the essentials; and those essentials are different for different people. For some – for many, perhaps – it is all about the lyrics. For me, it is all about the melodies and the music; its form, its timbres, its arrangements. *A Saucerful Of Secrets,* absent from the Bluesky list, is a piece of music that in my mind has a significance far outweighing that of *Have A Cigar* or *Run Like Hell.* The *Atom Heart Mother* suite obscures *Sorrow* and *One Of These Days* as if with the glory and complexity of storm clouds hiding lesser atmospheric wisps. But, that is just my personal opinion. I had immense fun thinking about my top 20, and it served as a valuable research method when it came to finishing up this book. That my top 20 is different to the massed top 20 is surely a matter of interest to a few at least, which I, and fans anywhere, can discuss until the Holstein cows come home.

Bibliography & Resources

Festivalized, Ian Abrahams & Bridget Wishart, Gonzo Distribution, 2015.
The Act You've Known All These Years, Clinton Heylin, Canongate Books, 2007.
Revolution In The Head, Ian Macdonald, Vintage, 2008.
Inside Out, Nick Mason, Weidenfeld & Nicholson, 2017.
The Language Puzzle, Steven Mithen, Profile Books, 2024.
John Peel Margrave Of The Marshes, John Peel, Corgi, 2006.
Albion Dreaming, Andy Roberts, Marshall Cavendish Editions, 2008.
John Peel, Mick Wall, Orion, 2012.

Magazines & Websites
David Bowie quote – *Musician*, July 1990.
David Gilmour, Absolute Radio, on inter-group relationships – https://youtu.be/l13fRD_
hiP0?si=1FMh_a1-u90MudAg
Roger Waters quotes – *The Daily Telegraph*, 8 February 2023.